Praise for *Happiness First*

I won't spoil the plot of this book, but I will say this: Jackson has found a brilliantly original way of landing some timeless truths. Imagine a Dickens-style moral reckoning meets courtroom drama, built around 14 everyday misdemeanours that, if we're honest, we're all guilty of. It's clever. It's uncomfortable when it hits close to home. And that's precisely why it works.

—Dr. Andy Cope
Speaker and Co-author of Happiness Revolution

Happiness First is a book with heart. Jackson Ogunyemi writes with candour and courage about something many high-performing professionals recognise but rarely name: the quiet erosion of joy beneath the noise of success.

For leaders, teachers, entrepreneurs, and anyone who finds themselves busy but not fulfilled, this book holds up a mirror, and then very helpfully offers us tools.

Jackson's book is generous, practical, and deeply human.

A timely reminder that happiness is not self-indulgence. It is the foundation from which we do our best work.

—Mary Myatt
Education Writer and Speaker

Happiness First is both a recognition and a release for those who carry responsibility for others. Its exploration of the inner voices we all navigate reminds us that leadership is not about silencing them but knowing when each should be heard. The book invites us to press pause, take perspective, and practise intentional self-care so we can lead with clarity.

Ultimately, this is more than a book, it's a steady companion for anyone seeking to lead and live with greater well-being and purpose.

—Claire Ferens
Executive Principal and Regional Director

Happiness First is not only a joy to read, but also an incredibly valuable toolkit that you can use to introduce more happiness to your life by making small, sustainable changes to your days. The "greenhouse moments" concept really resonated with me and it's one I've embraced to bring a bit more joy to every day.

—Katherine Lewis
Editor

Happiness First is an honest, compassionate wake-up call for anyone who looks successful on the outside but feels depleted within. Jackson writes with courage, humour, and clarity, inviting us to confront the habits that steal our joy and rebuild a life rooted in self-awareness, boundaries, and joyful resilience. This book doesn't shout at you, it walks alongside you, reminding you that joy and happiness are not a luxury, but a responsibility. 🐾

—Samantha Stimpson
Founder & CEO
SLS 360
Inclusion Consultants

I thoroughly enjoyed the original style of *Happiness First*. Jackson unpacks the 14 costly habits impeding our joy and then invites us on a journey to rediscover that joy in our everyday lives.

—Debbie Williams
Marketing Director

HAPPINESS

FIRST

JACKSON OGUNYEMI

HAPPINESS

14 HABITS DRAINING YOUR JOY
(AND HOW TO RECLAIM IT)

CAPSTONE
A Wiley Brand

Registered Offices
John Wiley & Sons, Inc., 111 River Street, Hoboken, NJ 07030, USA
John Wiley & Sons Ltd, New Era House, 8 Oldlands Way, Bognor Regis, West Sussex, PO22 9NQ, UK

For details of our global editorial offices, customer services, and more information about Wiley products visit us at www.wiley.com.

The manufacturer's authorized representative according to the EU General Product Safety Regulation is Wiley-VCH GmbH, Boschstr. 12, 69469 Weinheim, Germany, e-mail: Product_Safety@wiley.com.

Wiley also publishes its books in a variety of electronic formats and by print-on-demand. Some content that appears in standard print versions of this book may not be available in other formats.

Library of Congress Cataloging-in-Publication Data is Available:

ISBN 9781907312830 (Cloth)
ISBN 9781907312847 (ePub)
ISBN 9781907312854 (ePDF)

Cover Design: Wiley
Cover Image: © akinbostanci/Getty Images

Set in 11/14.5 pt and Bembo Std by Straive, Chennai, India
Printed and bound by CPI Group (UK) Ltd, Croydon, CR0 4YY

C9781907312830_070526

*This book is dedicated to **you**.*

To your journey.

To the impact you are choosing to make on yourself.

And to the ripple effect that impact will have on the world around you.

Thank you for picking up this book.

This dedication is for you.

Contents

Foreword

The Man. The Book. The Message.

If you've never attended an Action Jackson keynote or seminar, you should. It's an experience that stays with you. The smile. The energy. The sense that you've been plugged directly into the mains. You leave buzzing.

I've also had the pleasure of getting to know Jackson off stage and, truth be told, he's not that different. When the showman's hat comes off, the radiance remains. He's fuelled by faith, purpose, and two young daughters who clearly keep him grounded in what really matters.

I won't spoil the plot of this book, but I will say this: Jackson has found a brilliantly original way of landing some timeless truths. Imagine a Dickens-style moral reckoning meets courtroom drama, built around 14 everyday misdemeanours that, if we're honest, we're all guilty of. It's clever. It's uncomfortable when it hits close to home. And that's precisely why it works.

As for the subject matter . . . what can I say? I've spent the best part of two decades researching the science of happiness and human flourishing, culminating in around 130,000 words of academic turgidity. This book says much of the same thing, without the waffle. We've approached the subject from different ends of the telescope but have seen the exact same thing!

The world's got its knickers in a twist. We've become a human *race* in the most literal sense: a lung-busting sprint through life where busyness is worn as a badge of honour and happiness has quietly slipped out the back door.

And yet it's the one thing we all want more of. Ask yourself: If you could wish just one thing for your children, what would it be? Success? Money? Security? Scratch beneath the surface and the answer is always the same – happiness. In fact, I'd go further. Happiness isn't just one goal among many; it's the goal behind all your other goals.

The fact that Jackson is a good man with a big heart (and an even bigger smile) is reason enough to pick up this book. The fact that it has such an original premise is a reason to give it your time. And the fact that it puts happiness front and centre is a reason to absorb every word.

Thank you, Jackson, for doing what you do. This, my friend, is legacy territory.

—Dr. Andy Cope
Keynote speaker, author, and well-being researcher.

Acknowledgements

I would like to sincerely acknowledge the team at **Wiley – Annie, Stacey, and Alice** for their consistent support throughout the journey of bringing this book to life. It has truly been a journey and a half, and I'm grateful that we are here together at this moment.

To the team at **Write Business Results**, thank you so much. And to **George, Katherine, and Georgia**, thank you for your commitment, professionalism, and support along the way.

To all my colleagues who featured in the **Happiness Hall of Fame**, thank you for being living examples of what happiness looks like in a busy world. Your stories, perspectives, and lived joy brought this work to life.

To my darling wife, **Nancy**, thank you for making me feel loved and for being a strong spiritual support, allowing me to walk freely and live happily, and to my two girls, **Olivia and Yadah**, you are the epitome of happiness. I acknowledge you for the support you have given to this book and for the moments you have created that have taught me some of life's greatest lessons. Thank you.

Thank you all.

Introduction

The Wake-Up Call I Didn't See Coming

It's 10:30 p.m. The kind of silence that blankets a hotel room at night and hints tomorrow is a big day wraps around me like a gentle weight. I'm in my room, winding down. The glow of the bedside lamp casting a soft golden hue on the walls.

My laptop is open. PowerPoint slides are still on the screen, the cursor blinking over the last bullet point. Tomorrow's talk is on "The Importance of Respect." I've been through it in my mind a hundred times.

It's more than a keynote. It's a seed. One sentence might change someone's path.

That thought makes me breathe a little deeper. I love what I do. But tonight. . . I feel something stirring beneath the surface.

I'm just about to shut down for the night when I hear it.

Ping.

A message lights up my phone.

"Where are you?"

It's JC, my brother, not by blood but by battle. My speaking partner. My confidant. A man who knows my rhythms and silences alike.

I reply: *"About to sleep."*

He responds instantly: **"I'm at the bar."**

And just like that, everything shifts.

You see, JC isn't just passing through. None of us are. We are here on assignment. A mission. A moment with purpose. But before the delivery came the download.

Also staying at this hotel are two more powerhouses: Kheron and Alim. Brothers I've built with for years. Men who've seen me onstage and off. Who know the difference between my confidence and my chaos. We were all gearing up to pour out the next morning but it turns out, we needed to be poured into first.

I close the laptop.

Slide into my trainers.

Throw on a hoodie.

And head downstairs.

The elevator hums. The hallway smells like a mix of industrial cleaner and travel fatigue. A couple laughs quietly near the vending machine. The door to the bar opens with a soft swoosh and a sudden warmth.

The lighting is low like it's asking you to be honest. You know that kind of light. The kind that invites truth.

People are scattered in quiet clusters. The sound of glasses clinking is like an irregular metronome in the background. There's muted football on the screen. A bartender polishing a tumbler.

Then I see him.

JC.

Leaning back. Watching the room. Present. Alert. Open.

I walk over. We lock eyes. We laugh before saying a word. It's the kind of laugh that holds years.

And then, the **man hug**; you know the one. The kind with the clasp of hands and a strong pull in followed by a thump on the back that says, *"I see you. I've missed you. Let's skip the small talk."*

No words needed. Just presence.

Before I can sit, he leans in.

"What you drinking?"

The large Coke with ice almost has me. But it's late. And sugar after 8 p.m. violates a rule I don't play with, my nighttime routine. No sugar, no heavy eating. (More about that later.)

So I choose clarity.

"Mint tea," I say.

Clarity over comfort.

Moments later, Kheron and Alim arrive.

Another round of hugs, laughter, a little ribbing. But under it all something deeper.

It isn't long before the masks drop.

We didn't gather to network.

We gathered to **feel**.

To be real. To admit that even as leaders, we carry weight. And sometimes that weight gets heavy.

We talk about everything: life, family, expectations, burnout, ambition. We talk about the emotional tightrope between high performance and personal peace.

Then. . . the conversation shifts.

We start talking about how we process the world. About distraction. Restlessness. The way our minds refuse to shut off. The flashes of genius followed by days of paralysis. The guilt. The doubt. The exhaustion.

I share how sometimes my energy is electric, like I could take on the world before breakfast, and other times it's like I'm wading through wet cement with no end in sight. How I struggle to sit still when my mind is on fire with ideas but equally struggle to move when that fire burns out and leaves nothing but ashes.

There's a pause.

That sacred kind of quiet. The type that doesn't demand a response. The kind that says, *"We see you."*

Then, in his usual light-hearted way, Kheron leans in with a half-smile, half-smirk, and says,

"You've got it."

"No way, bro," I reply instinctively, laughing it off.

"Do I?"

I look around.

The other two don't say a word. They just share that knowing smirk and a slow, deliberate nod.

I want to reject it. Push it back into the shadows. Because labels? Labels can be prisons. And I'm the guy who *breaks chains*, not wears them.

But deep down. . . I know.

If I am going to be free from the frustration, the stress, the shame I carry, especially in life and business, I have to confront the truth I've been dodging.

So I sit back in my chair. Silent for the first time that night. Mind racing. Heart exposed.

And then Kheron, gentler now, says it plainly, **"You've got ADHD, bro."**

The words didn't stab. They revealed.

I didn't respond immediately. Because part of me already knew.

I'd been living with this. . . *something* for years. ADULT ADHD.

I always told myself I just needed to be more disciplined. More focused. I thought maybe I was lazy. Maybe I lacked drive.

But deep down, I was scared of the label. I didn't want anything that made me feel *less than*. I'm the guy who motivates people. Who lights fires. How could I be battling something I couldn't even name?

Being neurodivergent is something that many people struggle with. As an adult it affects you professionally and personally.

The silence hangs as I process what's just happened.

Then JC, watching it all unfold, breaks it like only he could.

With a smirk and a sparkle in his eye, he says, **"You're not NEURODIVERGENT.**

You're neuro-spicy."

We burst out laughing.

And in that laughter, the shame cracked.

The guilt dissolved. The denial dropped.

That night, I accepted what I'd resisted for so long.

My procrastination wasn't laziness. My overwhelm wasn't weakness. My scattered focus wasn't a lack of care.

It was wiring.

And wiring can be worked with.

I just had to stop pretending I was supposed to be someone else.

That moment changed everything.

How My Drive Cost Me My Peace

This Introduction was born out of that night. A moment of looking into the hard mirror. A moment of vulnerability without shame.

I've always been a happy person. But leading up to that conversation in the hotel bar there had been a culmination of events, including significant financial challenges, that threatened to derail me. By looking honestly at what was happening, I realised I wasn't making the impact I wanted to any more.

That's when things got messy.

It was at the heart of that challenge that I had my first big realisation: I had been busy chasing money. While digging financial holes. But the intention behind my drive was not as pure as it should be.

My misplaced drive led to distractions. Which led to financial challenges.

That led me to a question: What if I'd focused more on my true intention? Would I even be in this situation?

But this realisation didn't hit me like a bolt from the blue. It crept up on me. It hid in the moments of silence when I was alone. Stalked me like my shadow. Became a weight in a backpack I didn't know I was carrying.

Until there it was. Staring up at me out of a bag of Co-op donuts. Coated in sugar. Looking inviting. But not a treat filled with jam. One filled with a promise for a better future. If I could break the habits holding me back.

Let me explain how I came to be holding that bag of donuts.

Every Friday, I had a simple ritual. Drop our family's laundry off at the launderette. Pop to the Co-op opposite. Buy a bag of donuts. Eat them all in one sitting.

But that Friday was different.

The donuts were heavier. I had noticed my habit loop of rewarding myself for going to the launderette with donuts. But I hadn't realised until then how heavy everything had become.

I'd stopped running or doing my workouts. I had a permanent headache.

Sitting in the car with a bag of untouched donuts and the scent of powdered sugar hanging in the air I knew I needed to make a change. To break these patterns.

It started with donuts. But it led to so much more.

That so much more is what I'm sharing with you in these pages.

I want to give you, the reader, an authentic path to joy, something that helps you reflect well without shame or guilt. I want to give you a way to regain your peace.

Understanding My ADHD

The conversation with JC, Kheron and Alim was a standout moment because it made me realise that I was living with a lot of pressure. And that this could be the root of some of the challenges I was facing.

I thought I was dealing with things, but I didn't know I was wired differently. All of a sudden, as what JC said sunk in, I started to understand why my outcomes were different to other people's.

That moment came with relief. And the relief of a lot of shame and guilt.

I'd spent years resisting labels.

But naming it, saying "I have ADHD" was like naming my adversary.

Now I knew what I was dealing with. I wasn't in denial any more.

I could see that my ADHD might have caused me challenges. But it also brought incredible gifts.

Every night when I'm lying in bed, the brightest colours fill my head.

I have an unlimited amount of ideas.

I'm fearless when it comes to adventure.

When it comes to something new, I'm all in. And I'm very connected to people because of that drive.

I know that I've benefited from my ADHD far more than it's hindered me over the years.

But the struggle can be real.

Writing this for you has been a challenge because of the way my brain processes information. I didn't type this book. I **spoke** it. I used voice typing. Because if I'd sat down to write, my typing speed that's slower than a drunk snail would frustrate me and I would've ended up procrastinating over the opportunity to share this with you. But I found a way that supports me. It's a way that allows productivity to flow, which leads to more joy and less frustration.

This is what I want for you. I want you to find a system, an idea, a new way that works with who you are. Because when you find systems that work **with** who you are, instead of pretending to be what you are not. . .

You unlock freedom.

This applies whether you have ADHD or not. We're often afraid to accept labels of any kind because we fear they make us **imperfect**. We're all trying so hard to keep up this image of perfection that it's killing us inside. Slowly. We're competing to achieve the impossible. And it's the death of so many people's souls.

Chasing perfection is like eating candyfloss.

It looks huge from the outside. But you will eat and eat and eat. . .and it will never fill you up. But we want more, more, more. The more sugar we consume, the more it contaminates our system. It's toxic.

Chasing perfection – the perfect house, the perfect job, the perfect family – is like feeding your soul candyfloss. There's no nourishment. It leads to sadness. Then anger. Then depression. Then emptiness.

You become an empty shell.

But there is a way to breathe life back into your soul. It's simple. But it's hard. **Be still**. Sit in silence. Real silence. No music. No podcasts. Nothing to drown out what your heart is trying to tell you. Sit in the mess. Meditate instead of medicating.

Listen to the truth of your soul. I know it's not easy. I've been where you are. Avoiding that place. Hiding from myself. Scared of listening to the truth because I didn't know how to deal with what I'd hear. But trust me when I say that getting over that hump leads to so much more.

I found my truth. Felt vulnerable with it. And now I want you to find yours. If you're reading this feeling like you're trapped on a merry-go-round and can't get off. Spinning through your days in a blur. Not feeling or enjoying life. Get off. Stop moving. Is jumping into stillness scary? Yes. Is it worth it? Definitely.

Think about what avoiding your truth has already cost you. In your relationships. Your health. Your finances. Your self-esteem.

Now get off the merry-go-round. Stop. And prepare to take the next steps on your journey.

Welcome to the F.A.T Journey

F.A.T: Freedom. Authenticity. Transparency. (My ADHD brain just came up with that. That's one of the advantages, it's super creative. Anyway, back to my point.) Freedom is the end goal. It's what you're here to find. But you have to be very authentic throughout that process. When I say authentic, I mean being completely honest about who you are and where you're at. Which leads to transparency. You have to be fully transparent otherwise this won't work.

Our true North is freedom. That's how I feel right now as I'm writing these words. But being authentic has not been straightforward. Sometimes I feel myself moving in the wrong direction. That's when I course correct with transparency. I'm not saying you have to share your story with the world, as long as you share it with yourself. All of it.

If these three concepts appeal to you, read on. . . If not, put this book down and continue to pretend that everything is OK while you struggle and suffer in silence with your lack of total joy and fulfilment in life. Ouch! Who said that. . . Whoops! That's coach Jackson, a version of me you'll get to meet throughout this book. He is the no BS no excuse guy. While we're here I might as well introduce you to the cast of the *Happiness First* book.

These are the five individuals you'll meet as you flip through the pages of this book. Actually, before we go any further, I need to warn you: This book comes with voices.

No, not *those* kinds of voices. I'm not schizophrenic, I'm just expressive.

You see, as you turn these pages, you're going to hear me switch tones. A lot. One moment I'm inspirational, the next I'm lecturing, then I'm your biggest cheerleader, and two pages later I'm roasting you lovingly like a Sunday lamb shank. And it's all intentional.

Why? Because life requires different voices. And so does transformation.

Over the years, I've come to realise that we all need **five key voices** in our lives to help us grow, stretch, and evolve. And in this book, you'll meet them all. Sometimes separately, sometimes all at once. So let me introduce the cast:

1. The Motivator – The Voice of Why

This is the voice that ignites your fire. The "You've got this!" The TED Talk. The Beyoncé beat drop. The motivator is here to pull you out of the pit and remind you of your *why*. Big vision. Purpose. Legacy. Let's go!

Expect this voice when I'm trying to lift you out of your comfort zone and throw you into your calling. Don't fight it. Just let the goose-bumps do their thing.

2. The Coach – The Voice of How

This one's all business. No fluff. No sugar-coating. The coach is obsessed with results. They will challenge you. Push you. Sometimes offend you. But they do it because they see something great in you.

When you hear this voice, grab your notebook or your excuses and let's go to work.

3. The Educator – The Voice of What

Ah, the wise one. The teacher. The one with the diagrams and bullet points. This voice brings you principles, frameworks, studies, ideas and sometimes sciencey stuff (like cortisol and atrophy).

This is where you learn the *what* and the *why it matters*. Don't skip it; this is where depth lives.

4. The Friend – The Voice of Who

Now this voice? Warm. Comforting. The friend makes you feel seen, heard, and safe. They tell you it's okay to not be okay. They'll sit with you in the mess and remind you that you're not alone.

Friendship is powerful. It gives us belonging. But friends also tell you when your breath stinks or your life choices need a revamp. That's real love.

5. The Entertainer – The Voice of Soul

Here comes the joker. The storyteller. The one who makes you laugh and cry in the same sentence. The entertainer keeps your soul engaged. Because growth without joy is just a burden.

Expect punchlines. Expect rhythm. Expect me breaking into silent disco flashbacks or comparing your work-life balance to burnt toast. That's how I roll.

Why These Voices Matter

Sometimes, the friend will comfort you. But you'll also need the coach to stretch you. The motivator to fire you up. The educator to ground you. And the entertainer to keep you sane.

In your own life, you'll notice these voices coming through in different relationships. Sometimes they're external: your boss, your mentor, your best friend. And sometimes, these voices are internal: your intuition, your conscience, your inner hype-man.

The goal is *not* to pick one and stick to it. The goal is to integrate all five. To *become* them. And to recognise when each one needs to take the mic.

So if you feel like the tone is switching throughout this book, you're absolutely right.

Because healing isn't linear.

Transformation isn't monotone.

And happiness. . . happiness needs a full choir.

So Who Is This Book For?

If you're a high-achiever secretly running on empty. . .

If you manage people, teams, or high-stakes projects and feel like you're holding it all together with chewing gum and hope. . .

If you're in a fast-paced sector like finance, wellness, coaching, e-commerce and the speed is stealing your soul. . .

If you crave joy, balance and meaning, but feel like a prisoner to your calendar. . .

Then this book is your mirror.

You've mastered the art of appearing successful while quietly suffocating.

You've become fluent in the language of burnout, wearing exhaustion like it's a badge of honour.

And if you're finally ready to trade that for something deeper, welcome. You've found your tribe.

Before you read any further, ask yourself this question: *"What would your 70-year-old self say to you now about the way you're living your life?"*

Something popped into your head immediately. I know it.

Maybe you want to push that thought away. Please don't.

This question helps us escape what's known as Solomon's Paradox. You see, Solomon was a wise man, but he didn't follow his own advice in certain areas of his life, even though he could give excellent advice to those around him. Does that sound familiar? Solomon's Paradox refers to the fact that he was too close to his own life to see what changes he needed to make. We all inhabit this paradox.

The best way out of it, so I've heard, is to answer that question: *"What would your 70-year-old self say to you now about the way you're living your life?"*

Often we already have the answers we need. What we lack is the right questions to unlock them.

Why Listen To Me?

Because I'm not another motivational speaker.

I'm Mr. Wake Up Call.

When Google, Amazon, LinkedIn, and the NHS notice their best people burning out, they call me.

I don't deal in fluff. I deal in fire.

My "Wake Up Call" method isn't about feel-good quotes. It's about confrontation with compassion. It's about shaking you awake then helping you rebuild.

I've coached leaders, mentored entrepreneurs, and walked high-flyers from burnout to breakthrough.

If you want a dopamine hit, scroll Instagram.

If you want transformation? You're in the right place.

Let's Be Real

You're tired.

Your mind's racing. Your joy's missing. Your spark is dim. You tell your-self you'll rest "after this next launch," or "once the kids are settled," or "when I hit that next target."

But secretly, you're wondering. . . *is this it?*

You're successful.

But you're also. . . frustrated!

Trapped.

Numb.

This book won't give you more to do. It'll give you permission to subtract.

To breathe.

To come alive again.

This book is a mirror that invites you to look deep into your soul. To see every part of your life. It's a mirror that won't go away. It will keep coming back until your brain starts to rewire. To deal with what you're facing. To lead you back to joy. To happiness. To freedom.

This book is a subtle punch to nudge you in the right direction, because your brain will resist ideas that make it feel unsafe. Your brain is designed to protect you. And that's what it thinks it's doing when it moves you away from discomfort. So consider this a sneaky way to get behind the brain's defences and help it start the process of rewiring for genuine, lasting happiness.

What You'll Get from This Book

So, here it is. This is what I'm offering you:

- Guilt-free boundaries that stick.
- A redefinition of success to include joy.
- Sustainable routines that energise rather than exhaust.
- Practical tools you'll actually use.
- A blueprint for a life that feels as good as it looks.

Imagine waking up excited, not just busy.

Imagine leadership that flows from joy, not duty.

Imagine feeling light again.

This book will get you there.

The SMILE Framework

Before you flip the page, let me introduce something that will become your compass throughout this journey.

SMILE.

It's more than a word. It's a framework. A philosophy. A path back to yourself.

- **S – Self-Reflection**
  Because you cannot heal what you're unwilling to face. We start here. Always.
- **M – Mastery**
  Master your mind, your strengths, your limitations. Master the truth of who you are.
- **I – Implementation**
  Knowledge is just potential. Without action, it's wasted power.
- **L – Liberation**
  Freedom isn't just financial. It's mental, emotional, spiritual and physical.
- **E – Environment**
  Because nothing grows in a toxic greenhouse. Your surroundings must support your evolution.

Each part of SMILE will be unpacked in this book. Each section is a wake-up call of its own.

You're not just going to read about these things. You're going to **live** them.

Because the goal isn't **information**. It's **transformation**.

So here's your invitation:

To lean in.

To ask deeper questions.

To unlearn the noise.

To remember what joy actually feels like.

There's more coming. So much more.

The tools. The traps. The truth.

We're going to uncover it all.

This is your wake-up call.

Let's begin.

AI Assistance Disclosure

Let's be honest: With my ADHD brain, this book would still be a collection of half-written notes, voice memos, and ideas scribbled on receipts . . . if not for AI.

Portions of this book were drafted with the assistance of an AI tool (ChatGPT by OpenAI). It helped me slow my thinking just enough to organize ideas, clarify complex concepts, and translate bursts of inspiration into coherent sentences without asking me to "just focus."

Every word was reviewed, shaped, and approved by me. The message, meaning, lived experiences, and conclusions are mine alone. I take full responsibility for this work, and I thank God for technology that meets a neurodivergent mind where it actually is.

# Act I

The Harsh Reality

🎭 Act I, Scene 1
The Trial

"You are hereby charged with abandoning your joy."

[COURTROOM – MIDNIGHT SILENCE]

You don't remember falling asleep.

But you're here now.

Somewhere between dream and judgement, sitting in the back of a vast, towering courtroom.

You were told to show up.

No reason.

No context.

Just one line:

> *"Your life is under review."*

You assumed it was a metaphor.

But this place isn't playing games.

The walls hum with authority.

The judge's bench looms above like an altar.

A single spotlight shines at the centre of the room.

Then:

JUDGE (echoing):

"Will the defendant please rise. . ."

You freeze.

Surely they mean someone else?

"You. Yes, you. Step forward."

You rise.

You walk slow, confused, exposed.

"State your name for the record."

You speak. Quietly.

"You are hereby charged with the following crimes. . .

- **Neglect of Self**
- **Suppression of Joy**
- **Chronic People-Pleasing**
- **Glorification of Numbness**
- **Voluntary Emotional Starvation**
- **Second-Degree Abandonment of Your Own Soul"**

"How do you plead?"

You stammer.

You laugh nervously.

"I didn't know. . . I was on trial?"

The gavel strikes.

"Let the witnesses speak."

WITNESS 1: Your Family

A partner. A child. A sibling. A parent.

Each steps up.

Eyes tired. Words soft.

"You were there, but not really."

"You were always talking to someone else."

"You told us we mattered, but we only ever got what was left over."

"You posted about family. . . more than you were with us."

WITNESS 2: Your Health

A hollow version of your body.

"I gave you fatigue. You gave me Red Bull."

"I gave you panic attacks. You gave me a fake smile."

"I begged you to rest. You punished me with ambition."

WITNESS 3: Your Emotions

Fragile. Dull. Stuttering.

"You stopped listening to me a long time ago."

"You learned how to cry in private and smile in public."

"You called it strength. I called it silence."

"Now you feel nothing at all."

WITNESS 4: Your Mind

An overused processor, frayed at the edges.

"You used to dream."

"Now you just scroll."

"You fed me noise instead of thought. You fed me fear instead of focus."

"You trained me to survive but not to create."

WITNESS 5: Your Spirit

Still. Waiting.

A whisper in human form.

"I was your peace."

"Your intuition."

"Your divine access point."

"But you traded me for busyness."

"For applause."

"For speed."

"You left the sacred. . . for the scheduled."

WITNESS 6: Your Future

Clean. Strong. Electric. Sad.

"I could have been great."

"But you never gave me a chance."

"You traded me for comfort. And now I'm vanishing."

The judge rises.

"Let the defendant witness the outcome."

The lights dim.

A screen lowers.

You see a funeral. You are shocked!

A closed casket. A familiar crowd.

Tears. Nods. Whispers of regret.

The camera zooms in.

And then. . .

The lid opens.

It's you.

Not bloody. Not bruised.

Just. . .

Empty.

Expressionless. Unlived.

JUDGE (final):

"The sentence is numbness."

"A life without joy."

"Death by a thousand silent yesses."

The gavel rises.

But just before it falls. . .

VOICE (calm, unshaken):

"Objection your honour."

A figure steps forward.

It's you.

But from the future.

Alive. Awake. Whole.

FUTURE YOU:

"This one's not finished."

"I've seen what they can become."

"I'm here to guide the journey back to joy."

"Give me 66 days."

"Let them walk the road."

"Let them earn their resurrection."

The judge pauses.

Then nods.

A gold stopwatch appears.

66:00:00

It begins counting down.

"Return in 66 days."

"Bring new evidence."

"Let joy be your defence."

The courtroom dissolves.

And you?

You are wide awake.

Guilty.

But given grace.

[FADE TO BLACK]

⊘ Mirror Time: *"The Real Sentence"*

💬 A note from Jackson:

That courtroom?

It's not fiction.

It's you right now.

Because these charges?

They aren't legal.

They're *emotional.*

Every "yes" you said when your soul meant "no."

Every fake laugh. Every avoided mirror.

Every moment you chose performance over peace.

Your life has been collecting evidence.

Your joy meter has been screaming for your attention.

You just didn't have a dashboard to see it.

Until now.

You've just been sentenced.

Not to shame.

Not to punishment.

But to **redemption**.

66 Days

Why that number?

I didn't pull it from thin air. It's not poetic. It's *proven.*

Let me explain.

A while ago, I was deep into one of my Saturday 10K runs. Headphones in, brain switched on, soul wide open.

That's when I stumbled across a book called *Atomic Habits* by James Clear.

Powerful.

It didn't shout. It whispered. It didn't promise overnight change. It showed me the *compound effect of micro-movements*.

The part that stayed with me?

📖 *"It takes an average of 66 days for a new habit to become automatic."*

Not 21. Not 30.

66.

Why?

Because your **neural pathways**, the roads your brain takes most often, don't just shift by information. They shift by **repetition, reinforcement, and rewiring**.

I repeat. They shift by **repetition, reinforcement, and rewiring**. Do I need to say it again for that stubborn part of you that knows, but refuses to comply with a life-changing truth. . .

I think I do. Your life will shift by **repetition, reinforcement, and rewiring**.

You are the product of your *systems*.

You are the result of your *rituals*.

Which means your joy isn't a mystery.

It's a **mechanism**.

It's built.

Or it's buried.

I'm not just telling you this because I read it in a book. I'm telling you this because I've lived this path. When I started this process for myself, I went through 61 days of stripping back. In my head. In my heart. In my body. I fasted on nothing but water for the first seven days. For the first three days, I thought I was going to die.

OK, that's a bit dramatic. I knew I wasn't going to die. But it was hard. I also knew that I needed to get the toxins out of my body to unclog my thinking and get my ego out of the way. The part of my brain that had been trying to protect me, but in reality was numbing everything out. This is not about habit formation. It's about who you want to become.

This is where most people slip up. They focus on the doing. They don't focus on the who.

Now here's the kicker. Most people don't even get to the doing.

Whenever I speak to audiences about this, I ask:

▌ "How many of you have read *Atomic Habits?*"

Most hands go up.

Then I ask:

▌ "How many of you actually *followed* what it taught?"

And suddenly. . . silence.

That right there is the epidemic: We're **educated beyond our obedience**.

We've read the books.

Heard the podcasts.

Saved the quotes.

Posted the memes.

But when it comes time to *build the habits that save us*, we go missing.

If you've ever read a book, nodded at every line, highlighted every quote. . . and then gone back to your old patterns the next day, you're not broken.

You're *wired* that way.

And that's exactly the problem.

I've spent years listening to neuroscience giants; people like **Dr. Joe Dispenza** and others who've spent thousands of hours digging into the most important machine in the world:

Your mind.

And if there's one line they all echo, it's this:

▌ **"Neurons that fire together, wire together."**

In other words, what you *repeat*. . . you *reinforce*.

So let me break this down:

We are the **sum total of our habits**.

Habits are formed by our **thoughts**.

Thoughts are formed by our **neural pathways**.

And if those pathways were carved by stress, survival, people-pleasing, shame. . . guess what?

They're the roads your brain will *automatically* take. Even when your soul's screaming for something new.

That's why you need the courtroom, to make you confront what you've become: a zombie moving through life. Your brain, just like mine, is motivated to act based on pleasure or pain. You do everything you can to move away from pain and towards pleasure. But sometimes you need pain to get to real pleasure. You need to interrupt your brain and teach it another way of thinking. Of being. Of becoming.

But you also need purpose to work through the necessary pain. Your *why* has to be stronger than the pull of your ingrained habits. But you can train your brain to focus on this too. All you have to do is remind yourself, every day, *why you are going through this process.*

Remind yourself who is going to benefit from this. You. Your family. Your health. Your emotions. Your mind. Your spirit. Your future.

You don't lack desire.

You lack *rewiring*.

And so, if you're serious about joy, you've got to become a **neuroscience engineer**. This is how you escape from the voluntary starvation of your soul.

▲ *The 4A Pyramid of Transformation*

Let me show you how change really works.

Picture a pyramid with four levels – bottom to top:

1. **Accumulate** – You consume. Books. Podcasts. Quotes. Reels.
2. **Assimilate** – You begin to understand. The knowledge settles. Makes sense.
3. **Apply** – You take action. Imperfect. Messy. Real.
4. **Achieve** – You feel the change. You build momentum. You transform.

Most people live in the bottom two layers. They accumulate and assimilate **but never apply**. Why?

Because the brain **won't let them** unless they force it to.

Your current habits are *wired in*.

Your job now is to **rewire them out**.

This is where the **66 days** comes in. Not as a motivational gimmick, but as a **neural renovation timeline**.

Because. . .

Transformation doesn't happen when you read.

It happens when you *repeat*.

I'll say that again. . .

Transformation doesn't happen when you read.

It happens when you *repeat*.

When you push through the friction.

When you stop negotiating with excuses.

When you tell your nervous system: *we're going a new way now.*

So from this point forward, this book isn't just a script. It's your **rewiring manual**.

Every act. Every character. Every question. Every challenge.

They're all part of your blueprint.

To not just think differently, but to **live** differently.

You don't need more information. You need *repetition that becomes revelation.*

Let's rewire. One fired neuron at a time.

This isn't just another book. This is a **66-day transformation lab**. And I'll challenge you to **act**, not just to think.

Because:

Life doesn't change at the point of information.

Life changes at the point of implementation.

We're not here to collect wisdom.

We're here to *live* it.

So now you know why you've got 66 days.

This isn't a punishment. It's a process.

You've been sentenced. . . to *possibility*.

This book is your case file. Each chapter is evidence for or against you.

I'm not your judge.

I'm just your guide.

But your future self?

They're waiting. So let's begin.

? Journal Prompt

If you were put on trial for abandoning your joy. . . what would the evidence be?

Write it. Don't edit. Don't defend. Just get honest

Because this is Day 1. And this time, you get to rewrite the ending.

▐▜▛ Act I, Scene 2
The Guide Appears

"The journey doesn't start in the courtroom. It starts with a mirror."

[EXT. COURTHOUSE STEPS – DUSK FADING TO NIGHT]

The courtroom doors close behind you.

The sentence is clear: 66 days.

Not punishment.

Redemption.

You stand there, stunned.

The echo of the gavel still thumping through your chest.

Then. . .

VOICE (calm, familiar):

"Come on. Time's ticking."

You turn.

And see. . . **you**.

Not as you are, but as you *could be*.

Older.

Healthier.

Peaceful.

Clear-eyed.

Alive.

FUTURE YOU:

"We don't have long. And we have a lot to see."

[INT. WAREHOUSE – WIDE, STILL, SHADOWED]

You follow Future You into a massive, quiet space.

Concrete floor. No roof. Time doesn't move here.

Before you stand **14 doors**, each pulsing with a faint glow.

Each one holds a person. A version of a mistake. A lost piece of joy.

FUTURE YOU:

"Every door is someone you already know."

"Someone you've been."

"Someone you're becoming. . . if we don't stop the spiral."

You start to speak, but Future You is already walking.

[INT. THE CENTRE OF THE WAREHOUSE – A SINGLE OBJECT STANDS: A MIRROR]

Cracked. Yet still reflecting.

You step in front of it.

You expect to see yourself.

You don't.

You see **versions** of yourself.

The one who smiles through tears.

The one who lies and says "I'm fine."

The one who can't stop saying yes.

The one who forgot how to feel.

FUTURE YOU:

"You're not here to read a story."

"You're here to meet your patterns."

"To meet the parts of you that chose numbness over truth."

"This mirror doesn't show your reflection."

"It shows your *repetitions*."

You feel it now; the ache of all those repeated compromises.

"And now you're going to meet the people who've lived with your decisions."

[CUT TO A TABLE WITH OBJECTS]

On a table sit 5 objects:

- ⊘ A mirror
- ⚔ A Samurai sword
- ⌐ A hammer
- 🪁 A kite
- 🌱 A greenhouse

You reach for one.

YOU:

"What's all this?"

FUTURE YOU (smiling):

"These are the tools we'll need."

"But you won't understand them. . . until you've seen the 14."

"One room at a time. One mistake at a time."

FUTURE YOU (firm, kind):

"You're not broken."

"You're not too late."

"You've just been running patterns that aren't yours."

"My job isn't to fix you."

"My job is to remind you: **you already carry the answer**."

⊘ Mirror Time – *You Are the Solution*

💬 A note from Jackson:

This moment is everything.

This is the part most people skip not in books, but in *life*.

They leave the courtroom.

They get the wake-up call.

They cry. They vow to change.

And then. . . they go right back.

Why?

Because they don't meet the **guide**.

They don't meet the **future version of themselves**. The one who has already survived what you're walking through now.

And most importantly: They don't meet the mirror.

This mirror doesn't show you flaws.

It shows you *repetition*.

This next part of the book is where we get honest. Not in theory, in reflection.

You are not here to be inspired. You are here to be **interrupted**. To be called home. By **you**.

Because the truth is:

Your greatest role model. . . is the *Future You*, the you who made it through.

This version of yourself is wise. Future You carries wisdom that you've gained from falling and getting back up. From the scars that have healed. From learning the lessons that life has presented.

Talking to your future self allows you to embrace hindsight, foresight, and insight.

> **Hindsight** is where you look back and wish you'd done something different. "I wish I'd saved more." "I wish I'd taken a different job." Hindsight is powerful because we've got the evidence. We know how things went. We felt the pain of that decision. It's real. But if we become too buried in hindsight, we can't detach. We dwell on guilt and we get stuck. But when you can take the lessons of hindsight, accept where you are and let go of the guilt, that hindsight gives birth to foresight.
>
> **Foresight** is what allows you to see ahead. One of the lessons I've learned in hindsight around my finances is that I need to have the foresight to put 10% of my income in an account I don't see every month. I know Past Me not doing that caused me to have financial challenges. Which affected my peace of mind. Which affected my happiness. Foresight is all about learning from your mistakes and making changes based on what you learn.

Insight is your internal wisdom. It guides you whether your past, present or future self. It's always there. Like an inner compass. Too often, we ignore it. But if you pay more attention to your insight, you'll find your hindsight is more celebratory than regretful. Insight helps you make better decisions in the moment. The trick is learning to hear your inner compass when you're surrounded by external interference. The pressure to conform. To keep up appearances. To project perfection into the world. To chase dreams that aren't yours.

Who Are You Chasing?

> *"The only person I ever chase. . . is me, ten years from now."*
>
> **—Matthew McConaughey**

One day, probably while avoiding a deadline, I was mindlessly scrolling through Instagram. You know how it goes.

Then I came across a clip of Matthew McConaughey, standing on stage holding an Oscar. The moment should've been about Hollywood. Glamour. Gratitude.

But instead. . . he said something that *stopped me in my tracks.*

He was asked, "Who's your hero?"

And his answer?

"My hero? It's me in 10 years."

"Every day, every week, every year of my life, my hero is always 10 years away. I'm never going to be my hero. I'm not going to attain that. I know I'm not, and that's just fine with me because that keeps me with somebody to keep on chasing."

That speech changed something in me.

It reminded me that the most powerful version of ourselves *already exists.*

Not in the past.

Not in someone else.

But **in the future**.

We are all chasing someone.

Some of us chase our critics.

Some of us chase our parents' approval.

Some of us chase numbers, followers, applause.

But the only person worth chasing is **the you who stayed true**.

That's what this next part of the book is all about.

It's not about learning new information.

It's about *meeting the future version of you*, face-to-face.

And letting them lead.

Letting them remind you what you forgot.

Letting them point back at your patterns with grace and clarity and say:

"That's the habit that cost you."

"That's the moment you said yes to everyone but yourself."

"That's where the numbness started."

Because here's the truth:

You are not broken.

You are *buried* under repetition.

And this mirror you've just looked into?

It doesn't just show you.

It *reflects* every unspoken pattern, every compromise, every truth you're pretending not to know.

? Journal Prompt

What version of you is the mirror trying to show you right now?

Is it:

- The version that's burnt out, but pretending you're fine?
- The one that gives too much and receives too little?
- The one that hasn't rested properly in weeks?
- The one who is always "on," even when you're offline?
- The version who laughs out loud, but hasn't felt peace in years?

If you pay attention, really pay attention, your **future self will whisper the truth**.

So be still.

Ask.

Listen.

Write.

And remember, the version of you that you're chasing? They're already waiting. And they're cheering for you to get here.

I have recorded a short video for you. Log on to www.JacksonOgunyemi.com to get access to this video.

 # Act II
The 14 Costly Habits

In Act II, we're going to explore the 14 costly mistakes killing your joy. These are the pitfalls that slowly erode your life. Your joy. Your soul. They are the silent killer.

I was recently speaking to a room of leaders and shared the 14 costly mistakes with them. The shock on their faces was evident. At first it was funny. I presented it in my keynote as the 14 ways to ruin your life in 90 days. . . In stepped the entertainer. The one who would deliver the blow with some comic relief. The iron fist in the velvet glove.

So, what are these costly mistakes? Here's a preview before we re-enter the warehouse of doors.

1. Say YES to everything
2. Crave other people's attention
3. Cancel special occasions with family
4. Don't workout at all
5. Create time for toxic people
6. Overthink everything
7. Chase perfection relentlessly
8. Make a grudge list

9. Be guided by guilt
10. Buy personal development books and don't read them
11. Compare yourself to everyone
12. Complain about everything
13. Avoid delegation at all costs
14. Glorify busyness

Let's see how these 14 costly mistakes really affect your life. In each of the following scenes, you'll see a "Joy meter overlay." Think of this like the battery indicator on your phone. If your battery is low, it could cut out at any minute. You can't make an important call. You're desperately hoping the charge lasts until you can plug it in. Recharge.

Your brain has one of these indicators too. It tells you things. Lots of things. All day. Too often we wait until we're on red before we recharge. We're at 1% before we plug in. But it's too late. We don't have time to build back up. So we charge to 35% and rush out of the door. Hoping it's enough.

It's not.

Your brain is a tool. Your emotions are the underlying messages it sends. These feed into the stories you tell yourself. But you have to explore the underlying emotion instead of taking every story at face value. Sometimes that fear you're feeling isn't real. It's being powered by your amygdala. That tiny part of your brain that's hardwired to keep you safe. At all costs.

Sometimes your amygdala freaks out for good reason. You're in real danger. You're being chased by a tiger. Often though, in today's world, it's confused. It fires off to protect you from an email you find triggering. A phone call you don't want to take. An activity you don't want to do.

Understanding how your brain works and why your amygdala is in overdrive is empowering. It allows you to step back. Understand that it's trying to protect you. Examine your emotions and see them for what they are. Signs of discomfort. Not indicators of mortal peril.

Keep this understanding front of mind as you open each of the 14 doors.

It's time to go back to the warehouse, where Future You is about to begin the odyssey that will change everything. Fasten your seat belt. . . It's going to be a bumpy ride.

📖 Act II, Scene 1
Say YES to Everything

"Who needs boundaries when you can be everyone's doormat?"

🎬 **PRELUDE** – *Meet Your (In)Visible Influencers*

[INT. WAREHOUSE – JUST BEFORE DOOR 1]

You pause at the first door.

You're about to meet **Layla**, the one who said yes until her nervous system said no.

But before Future You lets you enter. . .

FUTURE YOU (serious, light humour):

"Hold up. You need to know who's actually been running your life."

"They're not on your payroll. You didn't vote for them. But they show up every single day."

"Let me introduce you to your brain's favourite cocktail party:"

Meet Your Chemical Crew

● Dopamine – *"The Hustler"*

"The feel-good hit that comes from ticking off boxes, getting likes, winning deals, or finishing tasks."

Think: *Emails, to-do lists, last-minute wins.*

Dopamine is the party-starter of your productivity.

Too much chasing it? You burn out.

Too little? You feel like nothing excites you anymore.

● Serotonin – *"The Peacekeeper"*

"The calm, stable confidence hormone."

Think: *Inner balance. Mood regulation. Contentment.*

Serotonin is the grown-up in the room. It doesn't shout, it grounds.

You lose it when you feel disrespected, unseen, or overextended.

● Oxytocin – *"The Connector"*

"The love drug. The trust agent. The social glue."

Think: *Warm hugs, close chats, eye contact.*

It's why kind humans feel safe and toxic ones feel draining.

Without it? You isolate, distrust, and scroll endlessly for false connection.

● Endorphins – *"The Painkillers"*

"Released during laughter, tears, movement."

Think: *Exercise, belly-laughs, dancing in your kitchen.*

They dull pain and lift mood.

Miss these, and life starts to feel heavier than it is.

⚠Cortisol – *"The Hijacker"*

"Your stress alarm. Helpful in danger. Harmful in excess."

Think: *People-pleasing. Overcommitment. Inbox anxiety.*

Too much cortisol? You stop sleeping, start snapping, and mistake survival for success.

FUTURE YOU:

"Now that you've met the crew, you'll see their fingerprints everywhere."

"Especially in this next room. . ."

🏠 Door 1 Opens: Layla – The Overcommitter

[INT. LAYLA'S LIFE – CHAOTIC DOMESTIC DRAMA]

The scene opens like a fast-forwarded episode of *Overwhelm: The Sitcom*.

Layla is everywhere.

She's:

- Typing a work email with one hand.
- Packing her toddler's lunch with the other.
- On speakerphone organising a bake sale.
- Smiling, nodding, silently dying.

Her house is filled with noise. Her head? Louder.

The doorbell rings; she apologises for "just being a bit all over the place."

Her friend laughs. "Classic Layla."

Joy Meter Overlay

■ ■ ■ ■ **Level: Draining Rapidly**

NEURO DASHBOARD

- **Dopamine:** ▲ Spiking briefly with each task checked off.
- **Serotonin:** ▼ Dropping steadily.
- **Oxytocin:** ▼ Flatlined – connection faked.
- **Cortisol:** ▲ Overload – the system is in "please everyone or die" mode.

[Scene shifts to a moment of stillness. Layla is alone, finally.]

She looks in the mirror.

Mascara slightly smudged. Smile slightly cracked.

She whispers:

"I don't even know who I'm being nice for anymore."

She sits down on the kitchen floor, back against the fridge. Her calendar pings.

She looks at her phone.

Smiles again.

A few seconds later. . .

Another ping. Another request.

A voice note from her sister:

> *"Hey Lay, I know it's super last-minute, but could you help me with the kids tomorrow? I've just got so much on, and you're always such a lifesaver."*

She stares at the screen.

There's a long silence.

The corners of her mouth lift just barely.

She hits record.

"Sure, I can help."

She sends the message. Still smiling.

And then. . .

She drops the phone onto the counter. Stares at it.

Something shifts.

Her smile fades. Her breath shortens.

Her eyes well up fast. Hot. Sudden.

And then

She breaks.

A stifled sob escapes her throat.

She **throws the phone across the kitchen floor.**

It skids under the fridge.

She slides down the cupboard like her knees gave out.

Buries her face in her hands.

"Why do I keep doing this. . .?"

Cut to black.

You're back.

Standing once again in the warehouse.

The door behind you is now dark.

Still echoing with the sound of Layla's breakdown.

You're silent.

Future You stands beside you.

Hands folded. Eyes soft. Voice low.

FUTURE YOU:

"Does it look familiar?"

"Sound familiar?"

"Feel familiar?"

You don't answer out loud.

You don't have to.

Your eyes are wet. Your breath shallow.

You nod.

Slowly. Silently.

Because you've been Layla.

You've said yes when your whole body screamed no.

You've smiled through the spiral.

You've collapsed on the floor after the applause ended.

You don't need to explain.

Because this isn't someone else's story.

It's yours.

[JOY METER appears in the bottom corner: LOW | RED | BLINKING]

💬 A Note from Jackson

You're here now.
Not in Layla's house, but in your own memories.

That last yes. That last breakdown. That one time you broke apart, and no one even noticed.

This is what happens when **you hand your joy over to guilt**.

When you perform peace instead of protecting it.

You can't heal what you're still hiding.

You can't reset what you keep rehearsing.

And you?

You've rehearsed people-pleasing so well, it's become your personality.

It's time to interrupt the pattern.

Layla didn't fall because she was weak.

She fell because she'd been holding up too much for too long with no one checking in on her, not even herself.

So let this be your check-in.

Why We Struggle to Let Go of "Yes"

When we say "yes" to others, we feel like we're creating a connection. We get a little hit of dopamine. We get the other person's approval. And we worry that if we say, "no" that the other person might reject us, or that we're in some way weakening our bond. We've framed our "yeses" as a way to get approval. But what if we're wrong.

When you say "yes" to every request, whether you really want to or not, you aren't respecting yourself or your boundaries. If you don't respect yourself, why should anyone else? A "no" isn't about not helping, it's about being respectful *of yourself*.

And let's examine that "no."

"No" might not mean "not ever." In some cases, it can mean "not for this moment, maybe later."

Someone saying "no" isn't a sign of rejection. Because it is about them, and not about you.

That means when you say "no," it is about you and not the person asking. We have to put a new frame around the word "no." One that says, "My no isn't about hating or hurting. It simply means I'm looking after number one."

And one "no" now might equate to five "yeses" down the line, because you have more strength to say "yes" when you give yourself that breathing space.

But ten "nos" might be followed by another hundred, because you're burnt out. But those "nos" are never about the other person. They are about you.

The Trinity for Saying "No" with Respect

If the thought of saying "no" makes you break into a cold sweat, I have a tool you can use: the trinity of saying "no."
Thank you.

Support.

Time.

That's it. Those three things. Here's how that might sound:

> *"Wow, I would love to. That sounds amazing. Thank you for the opportunity. On this occasion I'm unable to support you with my time on this as I'm doing a lot currently."*

Always start with "Wow." That little word releases dopamine in both your brain and that of the other person.

Telling them that their idea sounds amazing puts powerful context around it and you're thanking them for asking you.

Then you deliver your no politely, with context.

It took me a long time to learn this for myself. I'm a people-pleaser. I love giving. But I realised that the more I gave, the less respect I was giving to myself. As soon as I learned to say "no" without guilt, I became much more effective in all that I did.

My turning point in business came with a request for a booking as a speaker that was going to take too long and not pay enough.

I was busy. I felt like I hadn't stopped in weeks.

I said: "No, I can't do it for that time and price. I'd rather stay at home and play with my kids that day."

It felt great.

Reframing a "No" with Love

If you take someone saying "no" to your requests as a personal rejection, it's time for a reframe. Remember, their "no" is not about you. It's not a rejection of you as a person. It's their way of setting a boundary. Of saying they have too much on. Of respecting themselves.

When you find it hard to accept a "no," meet the other person with empathy.

Understand that your urgent isn't everybody else's urgent.

Look at them from a space of love and understanding. What else have they got going on right now?

Maybe them saying "no" is their way of building a healthier life for themselves.

Recognise that the other person might need a breather right now.

This is particularly important for leaders in any walk of life. If someone who usually takes on everything says "no" to a request, it's an obvious sign they're overloaded. But you need to see the signs before the "no." Build strong relationships. Recognise how much someone can give without breaking. Be sensitive to that.

And when you see someone who is doing too much. Saying "yes" to every request even when they're on the verge of burnout. Step in. Take something off their plate. Lighten their load.

Be transparent about why you're offering if they ask. Tell them you see how hard they've been working. How much they've been taking on. And that you want to help.

⊘ Mirror Time − *How Loud Is Your "Yes"?*

? Journal Prompt

On a scale of 1 to 10. . . how much of a "yes person" are you right now?

1 = I'm comfortable saying no and setting boundaries. 10 = I say yes to every request that comes my way.

Because "no" is a boundary.

And **boundaries aren't barriers; they're bridges back to yourself.**

📓 Act II, Scene 2
Crave Other People's Attention

"Because being deeply known is overrated – just go viral instead."

🎬 [INT. WAREHOUSE – IN FRONT OF DOOR 2]

You and Future You stand before another door.

This one is darker. Flickering like a faulty screen.

On the plaque:

▮ "Jordan – The Performer"

You hesitate.

FUTURE YOU:

"You've probably met Jordan before."

"You might even be living as him right now."

"This is the door where people don't fall from failure. . . they rot from applause."

"Be ready. This one's familiar."

🏛 Door 2 Opens: Meet Jordan – The Performer

[INT. OFFICE → RESTAURANT → BEDROOM → FEED]

Jordan doesn't walk, he performs.

Not tap-dancing or acting, but **in every room he enters**.

- In the office, he over-mentions his recent achievements.
- At home, he shares stories that position him as the smartest person in the room.
- At dinner, he's "present," but swipes his phone under the table.
- And on Instagram? Oh, he's thriving. Crushing it. Elevated. Enviable.

He has perfected the art of **curated identity**.

But under all that branding?

"Please notice me."

"Please clap for me."

"Please say I'm enough."

⚙ DASHBOARD OVERLAY

Metric	Status
Dopamine	▲ Ping-ponging with every like & view.
Serotonin	▼ Dependent on external approval.
Oxytocin	● Surface-level; no deep safety.
Cortisol	▲ High in quiet moments, post-scroll.
Joy Meter	■ Erratic. Looks full. Feels empty.

🎭 THE SLOW UNRAVELLING

We cut to Jordan lying in bed.

Blue light from the screen illuminating his face.

Everyone else is asleep.

His post didn't perform well.

He deletes it.

Checks someone else's win.

Scroll. Scroll. Smile fades. Scroll.

He turns to his partner beside him.

They're asleep. Peaceful.

He reaches out to hold their hand.

They roll away in their sleep.

He turns back to the screen.

Opens Notes.

Starts typing a new caption:

▌ *"10 lessons I've learned about success. . ."*

Then he deletes it.

And whispers to himself:

"What if I stopped pretending?"

Cut to a flashback:

A child version of Jordan.

Trying to impress his father after performing in a school play.

"Did I do good?"

"Were you proud?"

The adult Jordan is back in bed, crying now.

Silently.

Phone on chest.

Tears hitting the glass.

The final shot: Jordan stares at his reflection in the black screen.

And it doesn't look like him anymore.

[FADE TO BLACK]

🎬 **[INT. WAREHOUSE – BACK AT THE DOOR]**

You step out.

You're quiet.

Future You stands beside you. No words yet.

Just. . . watching you absorb it.

Then:

FUTURE YOU:

"Have you ever posted something. . . just to feel seen?"

"Have you ever performed peace. . . just to earn praise?"

"Jordan's not just out there. He's *in here*." Future You points at your chest.

You swallow.

You nod.

Because you've been Jordan.

Maybe. . . you still are.

💬 **A Note from Jackson: The Unseen Craving**

Not too long ago, I was preparing a sermon. One that focused on helping people tune out the noise of the world so they could hear the **still, small voice of God.**

The idea was simple:

There are many voices in this world. . . but only one Voice that gives life.

But as I studied, I found myself wondering, as I sometimes do, down an unexpected rabbit hole.

I stumbled on a video about something called **mimetic desire**.

I had never heard the phrase before, but as the speaker explained it, my jaw dropped.

Mimetic desires are desires we inherit not because they're real, but because we saw someone else chasing them first.

It's when we want what they want because they want it. Not because it aligns with who we are.

It's subtle.

It's silent.

And it's **everywhere**.

As I often do when I discover a new word, I dug deeper.

The word *mimetic* comes from the Greek word *mimesthai* "to imitate."

So *mimetic desire* is quite literally **imitated desire**.

We begin to want what others want because we've been shown it enough times that it begins to feel like our own longing.

That hit me hard.

Because suddenly, Jordan's story made perfect sense.

He wasn't just chasing likes or claps or accolades.

He was chasing a version of himself that the world handed him.

He became addicted to attention *not because it was true,* but because it was *offered*.

And that's the tragedy of mimetic desire:

It convinces you to abandon your joy in order to borrow someone else's.

It doesn't always show up in the form of chasing likes on social media. Sometimes it's as simple as buying that jacket you've seen five people wearing already this week. Or booking a holiday to that "secluded" island that every travel influencer has visited in the last six months.

This is how herd mentality starts. With mimetic desire. That's implanted in your environment.

It becomes very dangerous when you're surrounded by people who are attention seekers. That's how you end up like Jordan.

Recently, I spoke to a speaker colleague who was spiralling.

He told me he'd been scrolling through LinkedIn and noticed other speakers getting more attention than him.

More engagement. More bookings. More buzz.

And he admitted, quite vulnerably, that it was starting to affect his joy. His confidence. His sense of purpose.

That's mimetic desire. It sneaks in through the feed. Through the scroll. Through the applause. It *whispers*:

"You should be doing that."

"Why don't you have that?"

"They're ahead of you."

"You're behind."

And slowly, you stop hearing the voice of God.

You stop trusting the stillness.

You start tuning your soul to the algorithm instead of the Almighty.

Jordan is all of us.

Not because we are all attention-seekers, but because we are seeking connection. That's an innate part of being human. Centuries ago, a lack of connection and being cast out of society meant almost certain death. We are hard-wired to crave connection.

We can feel this craving most acutely after a breakup or a loss of a loved one. Anything that leaves a hole. A hole that you desperately want to fill.

Social media can feel like the answer. A quick-fix connection. But it's not deep. It's not meaningful. And it's never enough.

Here's the really scary part. . .

We don't even know we're doing it.

Because mimetic desires are **unconscious**.

They zombify us.

They erode our sense of direction until we're *running full speed towards something we never wanted in the first place.*

But now that you know the word, you can watch for the pattern.

This chapter isn't just about social media. It is about the **unseen craving for validation** in all its forms online, offline, in our work, our families, our friendships, our callings.

So before we move on, I leave you with this truth:

You don't need to be seen by the crowd to be known by the Creator.

He sees you. You are already enough.

Let's turn down the noise and tune back into that truth.

How to Tell If You're Chasing Someone Else's Desire

The only way to tell if your desires are yours or someone else's is to question them. Ask yourself, "Why am I. . ."
I went through this process for this book. I wrote my first two books for my ego. When I got approached to write this book, I paused. I asked "Why are you writing this book? Is it for your ego? Because if it is, tell them no."

The more I asked myself "why?," the more I was able to tap into my purpose rather than performance.

Question your motives behind the move.

Isolate or Insulate

There are two ways to escape the trap of mimetic desire once you've identified it: isolate or insulate.

> **Isolate** means you physically remove yourself from the environment. The second you do that, you protect yourself mentally.
>
> **Insulate** is what you have to do if you're in a situation where you can't physically remove yourself from that environment. In electrical terms, insulation can't conduct electricity. It contains it.

When you insulate, you're fortifying your mind.

Ask yourself: "Can I include myself in a healthy environment?" If the answer is "yes," do it.

If you can't, learn how to insulate yourself from the environment you're in.

When you're deciding whether to isolate or insulate, always come back to your identity and your mission.

What kind of person am I trying to become?

What is my mission in this life?

So, I know that isolating myself from social media is best for me personally. But I also need to use social media to share my mission for helping others find their happiness.

As a man of integrity, what does using social media look like?

It means if I say I'll post and then go before 12 p.m., I post, then go. No scrolling. No lingering on the app. In, write a post or upload a video. Hit post. Done.

That's what a man of integrity does. But yesterday I jumped back onto my social media to "just check something. . ." Then I started scrolling.

But I noticed.

I stopped.

I closed the app.

There's work to be done, no doubt. But every time I think about any part of my life, not just social media, it's through that lens: Who am I trying to become and what's my mission?

Visibility online might magnify your mission. But do it with intentionality.

◎ **Mirror Time** – *The Applause Trap*

? **Journal Prompt**

On a scale of 1 to 10, how much of your identity is shaped by the need for attention or affirmation from others?

1 = My mood lives and dies on applause; 10 = Internally anchored, audience irrelevant

Ask yourself:

What's the cost of constantly performing?

# Act II, Scene 3

Cancel Special Occasions with Family

"Nothing says love like prioritising work emails over birthdays."

🎬 **[INT. WAREHOUSE – IN FRONT OF DOOR 3]**

Future You stands beside you again.

This time, there's a pause before the door.

FUTURE YOU (calm, but heavy):

"There are some moments you don't get back."

"This isn't about failure or burnout. This one's about regret."

"The kind that hides behind good intentions. . . but still costs you everything."

You both look up at the brass plaque above the door:

"Mel – The No-Show"

"You ready?"

You nod slowly.

🔒 Door 3 Opens: Meet MEL – The No-Show

[INT. EMPTY DINING ROOM – 6:45 p.m.]

The table is set for four. Plates out. Balloons hovering. Streamers sagging slightly.

A child stares at the front door. Waiting.

It's their birthday.

They were promised dinner together.

They even picked the playlist.

[CUT TO: MEL'S WORLD – LUXURY, SILENCE, SCREEN GLOW]

Mel sits in a high-rise apartment.

Alone. Typing. Screen-glow dancing across their glasses.

A Zoom call is running. The topic? "Legacy Leadership."

On the screen, Mel says all the right things.

"People first. Values-driven leadership. Family matters."

They mean it.

They just don't *live* it.

Their phone buzzes.

A picture message: the birthday dinner. . . without them.

Cake half-cut. Candle wax drips.

The child is smiling, but not with their eyes.

Mel stares at the photo.

No words. Just guilt thick like fog.

They reply:

▌*"So sorry. Caught up with work. I'll make it up to you."*

But they won't.

And deep down, they know it.

⚙ DASHBOARD OVERLAY

Metric	Status
Dopamine	▲ Boosted by high-level productivity.
Serotonin	▼ Crashed from personal disconnection.
Oxytocin	▼ Minimal – no relational contact.
Cortisol	▲ Spiking from cognitive dissonance.
Joy Meter	■ Empty – success without intimacy.

❦ THE MEMORY LANE MOMENT

We flash through a montage:

- Cancelled recitals
- Skipped anniversaries
- Forgotten inside jokes
- "Sorry, can we reschedule?" texts
- Gifts posted instead of presence
- Apologies sent in bulk.

Then the funeral scene from earlier drifts into focus. . . But this time, it's from Mel's point of view.

No one is angry.

But no one's really grieving either.

They respected Mel.

But they never really *knew* them.

Final shot: Mel, in present time, sits in silence. No applause. No ping. No celebration.

Just the sound of their own breath and what could have been.

[FADE TO BLACK]

🎬 **[INT. WAREHOUSE – BACK AT THE DOOR]**

The door shuts.

You stand still.

Future You finally breaks the silence.

FUTURE YOU:

"You don't lose your family in one big moment."

"You lose them **one missed dinner** at a time."

"One birthday you reschedule."

"One 'I'll be there soon' you don't follow through on."

"Until one day. . . they stop asking. They stop hoping. They just. . . get used to your absence."

You lower your eyes.

And for a moment, you feel it.

That deep, aching loneliness that hides behind your ambition.

You don't need to say anything.

Because this story?

It's already yours.

💬 A Note from Jackson

Let's call this what it is:

Performative success is bankrupt without real connection.

You can win at work and lose at life.

You can gain the world and grow distant from the people who gave you one.

The sad thing is, we never plan to lose our loved ones.

We just keep *postponing* them.

Until "later" becomes never.

Here's the real problem:

We don't cancel dinner because we don't care.

We cancel it because we think we have *more time*.

But joy doesn't live in "later."

It lives in **moments**; the ones you've already rescheduled three times this month.

Success means nothing if it doesn't include the people you love.

So ask yourself:

What's it all for if no one's at the table with you?

I just came off a 15-day speaking tour. Back-to-back stages. Hotels. trains. Taxis. A blur of applause, lighting cues and fast food on the go. It took a lot out of me physically, emotionally, spiritually. And I'm thankful that I have the kind of flexibility now where I can *choose* when to stop and breathe. Because I knew what I was losing while I was out there:

Time. Presence. Proximity.

The things that can't be rescheduled.

Unfiltered Presence

My daughters are amazing at reminding me of what matters.

They don't write speeches or schedule 1:1s. They just show up wide-eyed and open-hearted – asking the same three things:

"Daddy, carry me?"

"Daddy, can I sit on your shoulders?"

"Daddy, can I have a hug?"

That's their love language.

Unfiltered presence.

And if I'm not careful, I'll miss it.

Not out of malice but out of momentum.

If you live to be 100 years old, that means you only get 100 Christmases. I'm 45 years old. That means I've only got 55 Christmases left. And that's assuming that I really do live to be 100. This is where the danger of Mel's story really shines. In the illusion that we always have more time. Until we don't.

We say, "I'll make it up to you. . ." But who says there's going to be a tomorrow when you can?

I'm especially conscious of this with my daughters. I tell people that every year, I get 52 versions of my daughter because she's changing every week. And it's incumbent on me to be present, see which version turns up each week and internalise it. Because you can't rewind to a previous version. And you never know how much time you will have left.

You have to create moments of unfiltered presence every day. They don't have to be large. They can be small.

This morning, I left the house to go and meditate. I drove up a hill and as I sat on the hill, I saw a tree. It was a beautiful tree. Beyond the tree, I could see the sun slowly rising. As I was looking at the tree, one of its leaves fell off. It arced and floated gently to the ground. I paused.

And I realised *this is the beauty of life.*

You can be invested in the future, but you have to remember the present is what creates the future. The life you're living today was scheduled yesterday.

That means you're scheduling the life you want to live tomorrow, today.

Paying into Your Emotional Bank Account

Yesterday, my wife was cooking dinner.
I was about to run to the office to finish writing this very chapter.

Then my daughter looked up and said:

"Daddy, can we eat together?"

I almost said, "Not now."

Almost.

But something in me paused.

And I said, "Yeah. Let's do it."

We sat, just for 30 minutes.

We ate.

We laughed.

We made up stories.

They fed me chips like I was a king.

They climbed onto my shoulders.

We bonded.

And in that simple half-hour, something happened:

A deposit was made in the **emotional bank account** of my children.

One that can't be matched by gifts. Or messages. Or reschedules.

Here's what I'm learning:

To a child, bath time is a **special occasion**.

So is dinner. So is sidewalk chalk. So is being picked up from school.

These aren't interruptions.

They are **invitations**.

And they expire quietly.

You don't need a weekend retreat or a two-week vacation to reclaim your presence.

Sometimes, all it takes is saying yes to **right now**.

That's what this chapter is about.

Not guilt. Not grief.

But **grabbing the moment before it slips through your hands**.

So next time someone you love says "Sit with me," don't wait for a bigger moment.

That moment *is* the moment.

You can make a conscious effort to start making deposits in the emotional bank accounts of the people you care about. Right now.

Tell yourself, "I will honour special occasions and special people in my life." That's it.

You don't have to spend lots of money. Honouring those people might look like making an Excel spreadsheet to remember everyone's birthdays. Or setting a reminder to send a silly meme to your best friend when you know they have a big day coming up.

The more you deposit into your relationships, the better. My wife and I made a conscious decision to have lunch and dinner with more people because we know we create strong bonds when we sit and eat together.

Instead of telling yourself you don't have time, ask: What would it cost to *not* do this? What will you regret not doing 20 years from now?

Here's a hint.

It's not sending that "really important" email.

⊘ Mirror Time – *The Ghost of Presence*

? Journal Prompt

On a scale of 1 to 10, how often are you present for the people who matter most?

1 = Fully available, consistently connected

10 = Routinely absent, emotionally distant

Now go deeper:

- Whose calls have you been "meaning to return"?
- When did your presence become something people have to schedule?
- What would your child, partner, parent, or best friend say about your availability?

Because presence isn't a gift you can keep in storage.

It only works when it's **given on time.**

📖 Act II, Scene 4
Don't Workout at All

"Fitness is for people with time. . . and self-respect."

🎬 **[INT. WAREHOUSE – IN FRONT OF DOOR 4]**

The hallway is colder here.

More sterile.

The door doesn't glow like the others. It pulses – like a tired heartbeat.

Future You rests a hand on the doorframe.

FUTURE YOU (quietly):

"This one isn't loud."

"It doesn't explode."

"It erodes."

"This is the door most people ignore. . . until they can't anymore."

The plaque reads:

▌ **"Chris – The Tired Achiever"**

🚪 Door 4 Opens: Meet Chris – The Tired Achiever

[INT. SMALL APARTMENT – EARLY MORNING]

Chris wakes up with a groan.

Not the cute sitcom kind.

The real kind – where your spine says "no" and your knees creak as you negotiate your every move.

He checks the time. 5:42 a.m.

He had planned to go for a jog.

Instead, he scrolls for a bit. Then closes his eyes again.

[MONTAGE – THE DAILY DECLINE]

- Hunched at the laptop.
- Late-night snacks to "get through this last task."
- Red Bulls replacing water.
- Promises to "start next week" that have lasted six years.

He knows better.

He even follows a few fitness influencers for inspiration.

But somehow. . . it always feels **just out of reach**.

His doctor recently warned him:

> "You're running on fumes, Chris. Something's got to change."

He smiled and said, "Absolutely."

Then opened his laptop in the car park and replied to three more emails.

⚙ DASHBOARD OVERLAY

Metric	Status
Dopamine	▼ Low – no reward system stimulation.
Serotonin	▼ Flat – no mood regulation anchors.
Oxytocin	● Minimal – isolation & screen time.
Endorphins	▼ Inactive – no physical exertion.
Cortisol	▲ Elevated – chronic stress accumulation.
Joy Meter	▮ Warning: *System depleted*.

🎭 The Snap

Chris climbs the stairs to his flat. It's only three floors.

By the second flight, he's winded.

His chest tightens.

He laughs it off, but there's panic in his eyes.

At the top, he fumbles for his keys.

And drops them.

He leans against the door.

"I'm 38. Why do I feel 68?"

He catches his breath. Trying to breathe through the tightness.

After a minute, he can inhale more fully.

Chris bends. His back complaining as he reaches for his keys.

As he closes the door behind him with a soft click, he turns and pauses.

Inside the apartment, a gym bag sits in the corner.

Still tagged.

Untouched.

Mocking.

"Tomorrow. . ." he mutters to himself under his breath. "I'll start tomorrow."

[FADE TO BLACK]

🎬 [INT. WAREHOUSE – BACK AT THE DOOR]

You step out of Door 4.

Future You is pacing slowly. Not speaking yet.

Then:

FUTURE YOU:

"Chris never meant to lose his health."

"He just kept telling himself he didn't have time to *keep it*."

You stand silently.

Because it's not about six packs.

Or gym selfies.

Or fitness trends.

It's about your **energy. Your aliveness. Your ability to show up.**

And when that starts slipping?

So does everything else.

💬 A Note from Jackson: The Shock Absorbers of Joy

A little while ago, I was on stage delivering a keynote. I was 50 minutes in.

The energy was high. The crowd was leaning in.

Standing ovation. You know. . . *the whole thing.*

We moved into Q&A, and the MC asked me a question that came from someone in the audience:

> **"Do you ever have bad days? And if so, how do you manage them?"**

I didn't even flinch.

"I have them *every day*. I just don't *experience* them every day. Because I've put shock absorbers in place."

Let me explain.

Shock absorbers are my *non-negotiables*.

They're the small systems that protect my joy – especially when everything else goes sideways.

And for me? That starts with **movement**.

Even on days when I believe I don't have time – when the calendar is full, the to-do list is aggressive, or my brain is foggy – I still move.

Why?

Because I don't trust my own brain sometimes. It tells me I'm too tired. Too late. Too overwhelmed. And I know. . . that voice lies.

So I created **a system**:

- A **1-minute workout** (for the days when I've got "nothing left")
- A **15-minute workout** (for a quick boost and reset)
- A **45-minute workout** (my regular go-to)
- A **2-hour workout** (for deep recalibration)

Each one serves a purpose.

Each one removes the excuse.

Each one says: *No matter what, I put me first today.*

Because here's the thing:

Busy people make brilliant excuses.

I know – I've made them all.

But excuses don't protect your energy.

Systems do.

And every time I move, even for just 15 minutes, I feel it:

My energy spikes.

My skin glows.

My soul buzzes.

My clarity returns.

My **joy wakes up**.

So if you're waiting for motivation to move again?

Don't.

Build a system that doesn't *need* motivation, just commitment.

Because when you move your body, you don't just release stress.

You reclaim your *aliveness*.

Let's get honest.

Most people don't *decide* to abandon their bodies. They just stop prioritising them, one tired day at a time.

The lie sounds like this:

"I'll start when things slow down."

"I just need to finish this one project."

"January. Definitely January."

But life doesn't pause for your excuses. And your body doesn't reset just because your schedule is packed.

I've seen it over and over – brilliant people *dragging* themselves through life, emotionally sharp but physically depleted.

They're not broken.

They're just *disconnected*.

Because here's the truth:

Joy lives in the body.

And when you disconnect from the body, you disconnect from the ability to feel joy – fully.

Why Movement Fuels the Mind

When you go to the gym. Or go for a run. Or hit that dance class. You create energy in your body. That energy pours out of you. But why does it work?

When you exercise, you're taking in oxygen, which makes you more alert and productive. I work out first thing in the morning whenever I have the choice for this reason. When you work out, your body releases endorphins and dopamine. As you know from our Joy Dashboard, you need both of these to create consistent happiness in your life. And, of course, when you work out you're building muscle and looking after your skeletal structure, all of which you need as you get older.

But physical resilience also leads to emotional resilience. When you're tired and drained, it's harder for your brain to access the power and capacity within you. Ironically, the less you move physically, the more tired you become.

I'm not talking about just being physically tired. I'm talking about mental tiredness. Brain fog. Feeling like you're wading through quicksand.

We all know that this is true. So why do so many of us skip physical exercise? I believe it's because too many people have lost sight of their mission.

I know I need my body to be in top shape to achieve my mission. That makes it easy for me to say yes to exercise. And I've created the system I already shared with you so that I have zero excuses for not moving my body every day. I know that even committing one minute every day is better than committing no minutes.

Here's the thing:

Too many people focus on **motivation** when what they need is **mastery**.

Motivation is what your sculpture will look like when it's finished. Mastery is the process of sculpting.

This all ties back into knowing who you're building. Who you're becoming.

When you commit to building *yourself. Your true authentic self.* Rather than creating the inspirational version of you that you think people want to see, making time to not only work out, but to look after yourself in every sense becomes a little bit easier.

And if you notice that you've skipped a workout? Move forward with gratitude. Gratitude that you *noticed* that you didn't exercise today. Acknowledge what you observe. Be grateful that you observed it. Understand that you are a work in progress. You're not perfect – no one is. Commit to exercise the next day. Even just one minute.

You don't need six-pack abs.

You just need to **feel alive again**.

You need your breath back.

Your stamina.

Your spine.

Your rhythm.

You need to move, not to impress anyone, but to remember who you are underneath the overwhelm.

Ⓞ **Mirror Time** – *The Body Remembers*

? Journal Prompt

On a scale of 1 to 10, how connected do you feel to your body right now?

1 = *Energised, grounded, physically present*

10 = *Sluggish, reactive, numb or disconnected*

Now ask yourself:

- When did I stop moving my body with love?
- What story have I told myself about "not having time"?
- What kind of life do I want my body to be strong enough to carry?

You don't need a gym.

You just need to start *showing up*.

Even a walk is a protest against the lie that you're too far gone.

📖 Act II, Scene 5

Create Time for Toxic People

"Nothing says joy like spending time with people who leave you empty."

🎬 **[INT. WAREHOUSE – IN FRONT OF DOOR 5]**

The air in the hallway feels thicker.

Laden with words and feelings left unvoiced.

The door has a slightly green glow. The kind of green that makes you think of radioactive waste.

Future You pauses. Hand hovering by the door handle.

FUTURE YOU:

"This is a tricky one."

"It's insidious."

"It drains your energy."

"On the surface, everything looks fine. But scratch the surface and it's anything but."

The plaque reads:

▌ **"Kelly – The Peacekeeper"**

🏠 Door 5 Opens: Meet Kelly – The Peacekeeper

[INT. A NEAT KITCHEN – EARLY EVENING]

A couple are having dinner.

They look happy. Talking through their days. Kelly is animated.

"So, I was thinking this Saturday we could go and take a look? You know, just to see if it feels like the right place. . ."

"Babe, you know I'd love to, but the football is on at 2 p.m. I promised the lads I'd watch it with them. You can come too."

Jay returns to his food. Kelly looks crestfallen.

Then she rearranges her expression.

"Sure, I mean, we can always look at that house another day."

[INT. A CLUTTERED LIVING ROOM – AFTERNOON]

Kelly sits in a small armchair. She's surrounded by a group of three women who are talking animatedly.

But she's quiet.

On the fringes.

"I think we should have a big bash for Kel's 30th!"

Another voice chimes in.

"Yes! A big birthday is always a great excuse for a party. . ."

The chatter continues.

A night out. Cocktails. Now it's turned into a boozy weekend away.

Kelly is still quiet. Ruminating.

"What do you think Kel? Brighton?"

Kelly smiles.

"I'd been thinking of just having a quiet dinner. You know, something a bit smaller. . ."

"Ahhh but this would be so much more fun. We can have dinner any time!"

She wants to put her foot down.

She wants to say no.

Instead she says:

"You're right. A big birthday celebration it is!"

She puts on her best smile as her friends' faces light up.

Inside she's wondering, "Why don't I ever get what *I* want?"

⚙ DASHBOARD OVERLAY

Metric	Status
Dopamine	▼ Erratic – spiked, then drained
Serotonin	▼ Undermined by subtle emotional attacks
Oxytocin	▼ Artificial – mistrust disguised as connection
Cortisol	▲ Chronic exposure to emotional toxicity
Joy Meter	■ Draining – daily leaks detected

🎭 The Snap

Kelly sits on the edge of a bed in a hotel room wearing a sequined dress.

Her heels are tossed to one side.

She looks at the clock. 10:30 p.m.

Who leaves their own birthday party early? She thinks.

She feels exhausted.

The door opens and Jay walks in.

"What are you doing up here on your own babe? You need to come back downstairs, it's just getting warmed up!"

He reaches a hand out. Encouraging.

"I just needed a minute. I'll be back down in five."

"I'll get you a drink. . ." he says as he closes the door.

Kelly flops back on the bed as it clicks closed.

"But what if I don't want another drink?" she says to no one but herself.

[FADE TO BLACK]

🎬 [INT. WAREHOUSE – BACK AT THE DOOR]

You step out of Door 5.

Future You is watching you. Observing.

Then:

FUTURE YOU:

"Kelly is exhausted."

"She thinks that going along with everyone else is what she needs to do to be happy."

"But she's not happy."

You nod slowly.

You could see it.

The way each interaction stole energy from her.

How every time she sacrificed her needs or wants for someone else's, a part of her soul seemed to die.

Because when you always ignore your desires, **you starve yourself of joy**.

💬 A Note from Jackson

Every time you say yes, when you really want to say no. You're training people how to treat you.

We all need to compromise in life.

But what if you are the only one in the relationship who's compromising?

That's when you feel the energy being sucked out of you.

Being empathetic and being a giver isn't bad. But you have to create another side to your character so you're not emptied of your giving.

So you don't become a shell of yourself.

A caring relationship is reciprocal.

I fill you up. You fill me up.

Toxic relationships normally don't arrive with a big bang.

They slide into our lives.

One request for a favour here. Another there. Never an offer to return that favour.

Realigning plans to meet their needs. Never considering yours.

And here's the big one: taking without saying "thank you."

If Kelly's situation sounded familiar, pause for a moment. Think of a relationship in your life that you want to evaluate. Ask yourself how many times that person has said "thank you." And, most importantly, *how* they said "thank you."

The other day, I was prompted to send money to someone. So I did. Not a lot. Just a little token. And he sent me a video saying thank you and how much he appreciated me. It wasn't a lot, but it really showed he appreciated me. This person is a giver, not just a taker. He knew that I would normally send a video instead of a text, so he mirrored that back to me. He sent me a video, knowing that's how I like to communicate.

Letting Go of Relationships with Grace

When you understand that you are a giver, but that there are limits, it might be time to recalibrate some of your relationships – or let go of them completely. You need to do this because otherwise resentment builds. But how?

With **grace**.

Start by appreciating yourself. And then protecting yourself by decreasing your interactions with that person. Reduce the number of times you say yes to that person. If you are going to give, don't give as deeply as before.

In the past, you might have gone ten miles for them. Now only go two. You're still doing something. But not giving your all.

Just as we learned with Layla behind Door 1, sometimes saying no means you can say yes more in the future.

And sometimes those yeses won't be for the person you've said no to. Sometimes they will be for someone else.

Or for yourself.

Sometimes you can change your behaviour and let the relationship recalibrate on its own. Other times, you will need to have a conversation with the other person. But keep it simple. Factual. And about you.

"I've noticed something about our relationship. And I'm feeling every time X is done, I feel a certain way."

By approaching the conversation in this way, you're sharing your feelings, you're owning them, and you're inviting a discussion. Often their response will tell you all you need to know. If the other person is balanced. Empathetic. They will acknowledge it. Apologise. Promise to change. Together you can recalibrate your relationship.

But if they respond with, "Shut up! What are you talking about?" That tells you all you need to know.

And if you decide to walk away from a toxic relationship, whether romantic, a friendship or otherwise, know that feeling sad is normal. You're mourning. That person has been part of you for a minute. It's okay to be sad for losing that. Don't feel guilt. Just know that the sadness, the mourning, is how your brain rebuilds itself.

It's rebuilding for what's next.

It's a death. Acknowledge it. Accept it. But know that this won't last forever. Unless you hold onto it.

Finding Your Safe People

Safe people are **fun, loving** and **challenging**.

But they're not loving you so much that they aren't challenging you.

They're not challenging you so much that they push you away.

They give a good balance of love and challenge.

And when they're not challenging you or loving you, they are fun to be around.

⊘ Mirror Time – Watch Out for Energy Vampires

? Journal Prompt

Who consistently drains my energy?

On a scale of 1 to 10, how much of your mental and emotional energy is drained by certain people in your life?

1 = Energised, clear, protected

10 = Exhausted, tense, emotionally depleted

Now go deeper:

- Whose presence consistently drains you? Write the names down. Don't edit.
- What patterns or behaviours trigger that drain?
- How often are you exposed to this energy? Daily? Weekly? Occasionally?
- What is it costing you – focus, joy, confidence, peace?
- What would shift if you reduced access by even 10% starting today?

📖 Act II, Scene 6
Overthink Everything

"Nothing destroys the mind more than high levels of assumption."

🎬 [INT. WAREHOUSE – DOOR 6]

This door looks different.

It's covered in **scribbles** – questions, arrows, red lines, diagrams.

It's a **conspiracy wall** built by the mind of someone who never stops thinking.

The plaque reads:

▌ **"Isaac – The Analyst"**

Future You exhales.

FUTURE YOU (sombrely):

"This isn't chaos."

"It's control disguised as intelligence."

"Inside this door, you'll meet someone who can explain everything. . . except why they're still stuck."

They motion for you to enter.

🏠 Door 6 Opens: Meet Isaac – The Analyst

[INT. APARTMENT – NIGHT]

The apartment is clean.

Silent.

Neat piles of notes, journals, diagrams.

Isaac sits at his desk, staring at a glowing screen.

He's been drafting an email for **47 minutes**.

Still unsent.

He retypes the first sentence.

Then backspaces.

Again.

He sighs. Gets up. Makes tea. Sits back down.

Still unsure.

[MONTAGE – THE PARALYSIS LOOP]

- Drafted business plan: never launched.
- Message to reconnect with a friend: never sent.
- Gym membership: still unused.
- LinkedIn post: saved in drafts for six months.

He writes lists.

Then rewrites them.

Then questions the order.

"What if I do it wrong?"

"What if they misunderstand?"

"What if I mess it up?"

"What if I'm not ready?"

His brain spins brilliant *reasons not to begin*.

And he's so smart, he's convinced himself of all of them.

☀ DASHBOARD OVERLAY

Metric	Status
Dopamine	▼ Starved – no completion = no reward loop.
Serotonin	▼ Anxiety-ridden from mental instability.
Cortisol	▲ Constant low-level activation.
Joy Meter	■ Drifting towards red – too many open loops.

🎭 The Snap

Isaac receives a message from a friend:

"Hey man, just checking in. Haven't heard from you in a while. Everything okay?"

He stares at it.

Types:

"Yeah, I'm good. Just been in my head a lot lately."

Deletes it.

Rewrites:

"Sorry I've been off. Thinking through some stuff."

Deletes it again.

Then?

Nothing.

He locks the screen.

And sighs.

"What's wrong with me?"

[FADE TO BLACK]

🎬 **[INT. WAREHOUSE – BACK AT THE DOOR]**

You're back.

And you can *still hear Isaac's brain* spinning.

Future You steps forward.

FUTURE YOU (gentle but firm):

"Overthinking is fear wearing a lab coat."

"It sounds smart. It sounds safe. But it's just paralysis with better vocabulary."

"The longer you stay in your head, the harder it becomes to move in your life."

You nod.

Because you've been there.

And if you're honest. . . maybe you're still there.

💬 **A Note from Jackson**

Overthinking is a **slow death** with perfect punctuation.

You never crash.

You just. . . circle.

You replay conversations. Rethink texts. Redo the plan.

Until momentum dies, and confidence erodes.

And then you blame yourself for not doing anything – without realising you've spent your entire day *trying to do it perfectly*.

Here's the trap:

Overthinkers don't lack intelligence.

They lack permission – to begin, to risk, to be seen in process.

Because the lie says:

"Don't move until it's right."

"Don't act until it's safe."

"Don't try until it's guaranteed."

But that's not protection.

That's **procrastination in disguise**.

You will never think your way into peace.

At some point, you must risk being misunderstood. . . in order to finally feel *free*.

Breaking Free from the Fear

Overthinking stems from fear. Fear that we're not ready. Fear that we're not good enough. Fear that we haven't achieved enough. Fear that we'll fail. But neurologically, when we keep rehearsing our fears, we feel a physical impact.

It's like you've got an anvil on your head. Constantly. That headache blinds you to opportunities and your heart and soul become starved of life because you no longer control it.

That's when panic attacks kick in.

The antidote to this fear is surrender. Surrender to something bigger than yourself. Surrender to life.

This is where you give UP (and soar, like an untethered kite) rather than giving up (and accepting your fate). I give UP by thinking like this:

1. I didn't create myself.
2. I slept overnight and I didn't consciously keep my heart, lungs, or kidneys going. Another force did that.

And I will constantly surrender to that force. . .

Because it's been working for 45 years.

Personally, I surrender to God, the creator. Because when I look around I'm in awe of the wonder of life.

You don't have to believe in God to surrender.

Just **surrender to the beauty of life**.

Another way I stay free of fear is to focus on decluttering. As I'm writing this, I'm looking at all the books in my office that I haven't read and thinking that I should get rid of them. I can feel myself shifting more towards a minimalist lifestyle instead of working to accumulate more things, because it helps my mental state.

And I've learned that accumulation can sometimes equate to a false sense of success.

Then there's **presence**.

Whether you're playing with your kids or mopping the floor.

Be present. In the moment.

Escaping Procrastination

To escape the cycle of procrastination you have to first understand what it really is.

Procrastination is your internal bodyguard.

That big, burly guy sees something and shouts, "Pain alert!"

And you run.

Instead, before you listen to your bodyguard, ask yourself a question: Is this real pain, or perceived pain?

But understand that most procrastination stems from overwhelm. Mental overwhelm. And that's painful.

I don't believe we have lazy people in this world. I believe we have a lot of people who are mentally overwhelmed by what's happening in their lives.

We procrastinate over tasks that feel too overwhelming right now.

I do it with finance tasks.

I'll have folders everywhere.

Bills stacked up.

It feels like a lot.

So I say, "Jackson, just take one bill and open that letter. That's your task for today."

Not 50. Not 15. Just one.

With that one letter, I start to build momentum.

If you believe the root cause of your procrastination is mental overwhelm, ask yourself this: Why am I mentally overwhelmed? Often it'll be because you're looking at everything at once. So break it down. Take one bite at a time – that's how you eat an elephant.

You have to focus on each step on the journey. No guilt. You can't tell yourself "I'm not doing enough" because you are doing *something*.

If guilt starts to creep in, ask yourself: Am I on the right path? Do I have a plan? And am I following it slowly?

If you're on the right path, there's no need for guilt.

If you're on the wrong path, well done. You've recognised it. Now you can put yourself on the right path.

After all, **would you rather be walking slowly along the right path, or quickly along the wrong one?**

It is easy to be hard on ourselves. We all have a mental checklist of where we think we should be in our lives. But is that the right checklist?

Remember mimetic desire. Is what you're striving for what you *really want to achieve?* Or have you taken on other people's aspirations and desires without realising it?

Here's a simple framework to help you overcome procrastination.

I call it **The Three Gs**. . .

Gratitude: When you feel overwhelmed, instead say, "I'm grateful I have a mouth and can talk about this. I'm grateful I have ears to hear what I'm saying. I'm grateful I have eyes to see what's going on." Gratitude triggers serotonin release in your system, which helps you be creative.

Growth: You're telling yourself that you're behind, but are you really? Write a Trophy List. This is a list of all the things you've achieved to date. This will create a shot of dopamine and help you realise you're not as behind as you might think.

Goals: What do you really want? What steps have you created to help you achieve those goals? Small steps are just as useful as big ones.

Here are three questions to get you started:

- What am I grateful for right now?
- What progress have I made?
- What small steps can I take next?

Those three questions will help you calm your bodyguard down and regulate your mental state.

Silencing the Mantra of "I'm not ready yet. . ."

Many overthinkers tell themselves they can't start *yet* because they're not ready.

I hear you.

I've been there.

But what's really behind "I'm not ready yet" is a fear of failure.

Here's the thing:

You don't have to be great to get started, but you do have to get started to be great.

The truth is you're going to make mistakes.

We all do.

But it's better to make those mistakes now than waiting ten years and still making them anyway.

We start. We fall. We move again. We fly.

It's a process. And it's a process we all go through.

I told myself I wasn't ready to write this book. I was overthinking it. But then. . .

I realised, *Dude, you just have to sit down and start.*

The second I sat down, ideas started pouring out of me.

Questions arose. I answered them.

When you start, you discover. And when you can surrender to that process you build trust and flow. You can prioritise faith over planning.

Because often the best ideas come to you when you're not trying. It's why people often say they have their best ideas in the shower or on the toilet, because they're relaxed and they've reconnected with the flow of life, faith and nature. Much of the stress you feel is because you're disconnected from that flow, faith and nature. So, come back to freedom. To liberation. **Surrender.**

There's a time to plan. But start with the flow and put structures in ··
place later.

⊘ Mirror Time – *When Thought Becomes a Cage*

? Journal Prompt

On a scale of 1 to 10, how often do you delay action due to overthinking?

1 = Decisive, intuitive, responsive

10 = Mentally looped, anxious, stuck in cycles

Now reflect:

- What's one thing I've been *thinking about doing* for far too long?
- What am I afraid will happen if I just. . . begin?
- What lie am I believing about "getting it perfect"?
- What would I attempt if I wasn't afraid of messing it up?

You don't need another draft.

You need a decision.

Thought without movement becomes torment.

Choose movement.

📖 Act II, Scene 7

Chase Perfection Relentlessly

"Because 'good enough' is a phrase for quitters."

🎬 [INT. WAREHOUSE – DOOR 7]

This door gleams.

Crystal clean. Symmetrical.

It even has a gold plaque – no rust, no scratches.

Everything about it screams *flawless*.

But Future You doesn't smile.

They stand a little straighter here. The air feels. . . tight.

FUTURE YOU (measured, soft):

"This is the most well-dressed breakdown you'll ever see."

"It looks like excellence."

"But it's actually exhaustion."

You read the plaque:

▍ **"Camille – The Flawless One"**

You hesitate.

Future You nods towards the handle.

"Let's go meet the girl who got it all right. . . and still doesn't feel right."

🏠 Door 7 Opens: Meet Camille

[INT. DESIGN STUDIO – DAY]

Camille glides across the office.

Pencil skirt. Crisp blouse.

Her desk is pristine. Laptop spotless. Nails manicured.

Her calendar?

Colour-coded.

Her inbox?

At zero.

She's *everything you'd want to be. . . on paper.*

But look closer.

She re-records voice notes five times to get the tone just right.

She rereads her emails out loud before sending.

She rehearses "spontaneous" social posts.

Camille doesn't just chase excellence.

She *chases flawlessness.*

And it is **killing her slowly**.

⚙ DASHBOARD OVERLAY

Metric	Status
Dopamine	▲ Spiking with short-term achievements.
Serotonin	▼ Eroded by chronic self-doubt.
Cortisol	▲ Constant – fuelled by pressure and image.
Endorphins	● Minimal – no play, no rest, no lightness.
Joy Meter	■ Appearance of success, absence of ease.

🎭 The Snap

Camille presents at a high-level board meeting.

Her report? Flawless.

Design? Stunning.

Delivery? On point.

After the applause, she walks to the bathroom. Locks the door.

She stares into the mirror.

There's a smudge on her mascara.

She wipes it away.

As she looks closer, she sees the lines under her eyes.

She leans forward.

"Why do I still feel like a fraud?"

She fixes her posture.

Flushes the toilet for noise.

Then walks out like nothing happened.

[FADE TO BLACK]

🎬 [INT. WAREHOUSE – BACK AT THE DOOR]

You return.

Future You watches your face.

FUTURE YOU (quietly):

"Perfection is the mask we wear when we're afraid our truth isn't lovable."

"You don't have to get everything right to be worthy of rest."

"Or joy."

"Or being seen."

You nod, tears rising unexpectedly.

Because *Camille is brilliant. But tired. And so are you.*

💬 A Note from Jackson: When the Picture Lies and the Truth Heals

Here's the thing about perfection:

It shows up *quietly*. And most often. . . on platforms.

I'm quite active on LinkedIn. I write. I read. I engage. And I've noticed something – something subtle but significant.

Our brains are pattern recognition machines.

And when we see polished post after polished post, highlight reel after highlight reel, success story after success story with no mention of the scar tissue underneath. . . We start to believe that this is the *standard*. Not just for content – but for *how we live*.

We begin to post only the glory. . . and hide the story. Because somewhere in our psyche, it says: "Unless it's perfect, don't post it. Don't show it. Don't be seen."

I was emceeing a brilliant entrepreneurship event a while back. One of the speakers, Ruth, was talking about **visibility and authenticity online** – how we show up in digital spaces.

Someone from the audience raised their hand:

"I struggle to create stories for LinkedIn."

And Ruth's response was *gold*:

"Creating stories isn't the issue. It's having the **courage to tell your real story**. If you do that, you'll never run out. Because life gives you material every day. It's the fear of being seen in your truth that makes people fabricate – and *that's* the exhausting part."

It landed. It stuck. And it stayed with me.

So in the middle of that very event, I decided to *test it*.

I had a photo of me – sitting at a laptop. I looked focused. Composed. Professional. It was the *perfect* Instagram or LinkedIn visual. The kind of image that says:

"I'm working on something game-changing."

"I'm building something meaningful."

"I'm deep in my purpose."

But here's what I wrote in the caption:

★"This looks like I'm hard at work, right? Focused. In flow. On fire.

Truth is. . . I'm procrastinating.

I've got financial admin I don't want to do.

I've been avoiding it for hours.

I'm overwhelmed. Frustrated. And to be honest – I just don't want to deal with it right now."★

That was it. No polish. No spin. No redemption arc. Just truth.

And do you know what? It became the **most interacted post I wrote that year**. Why? Because I stopped aspiring to be **impressive** – and started aspiring to be **honest**.

People don't resonate with perfection. They resonate with *progress*. With pain. With process. With *truth*.

So that's the invitation of this chapter:

- Not to post more.
- But to perform less.
- To show less gloss and more grit.
- To tell the truth, even when the picture tells another story.

Because **when you share your mess**, you become more human. More relatable. More free. And sometimes, the most healing thing you can post is:

"This isn't perfect.

But it's real.

And I'm showing up anyway."

That's not weakness. That's strength. Let's normalise it.

Embrace the Season You're In

I believe we all go through seasons in our lives. We all have a spring, summer, autumn, and winter. You might be in the winter of your life watching other people who are in the spring of their lives and when you don't acknowledge this, you can feel like there's something wrong with you. There isn't. You're just in a different season.

But too many people don't share when they're in their winter. In fact, they'll be in their winter but online they'll be pretending to be in their spring. They're doing themselves a disservice and making it harder for all of us to honour where we are on our journeys.

I've realised that if I'm in winter and I share that with others, it helps people to embrace their own winters without feelings of guilt. By honouring the season I'm in, I give others permission to do the same.

I invite you to think about the season you're in. And share it. Even if it's messy.

Especially if it's messy.

When I started being more vulnerable with what I shared online and showing people my world without trying to impress them I felt an incredible sense of freedom. I realised I didn't have to match up to any markers, I could just be.

And that's special because too many of us hold ourselves accountable to metrics, targets and KPIs in our lives that are largely of our own making.

I'm not saying those don't have a place. KPIs can be helpful. But they're not the *only* aspect of life we should be measuring.

As well as measuring your key performance indicators, also measure your **pain indicators** and **process indicators**.

Know what process you're currently in. If you're in a winter, understand that this will affect your performance. But instead of fighting it, accept it. Be gracious enough to measure your life with balance. Know that pain can affect performance – and that's normal. Keep asking yourself:

"What process am I in?"

"What pain have I gone through?"

"Am I in pain now?"

Because all of these factors will determine how well you perform.

These aren't just questions we can ask of ourselves. These are questions we can encourage others to reflect on too. If you're a leader, you need to put systems in place to help those around you identify what season they're in and have open discussions about how that can affect performance.

Because demanding high performance all the time isn't realistic. Instead you need to have a hand each person's pulse to measure their vitals, which will help you create a calendar of outcomes. There is a season to prepare and a season to launch. Know which one you and your people are in. Honour it.

It can be a challenge to detach your self-worth from your work. So here's a question to help you begin that process: *"50 years from now, when you measure your impact on the Earth with your family, what would you like to measure?"*

I know that I won't be measuring social media followers.

Or the balance in my bank account.

I'll be measuring how many smiles I saw on my daughters' and wife's faces.

How many smiles I put on other people's faces.

Because although short-term targets have their place, we shouldn't attach our self-worth to transient measurements. We need to measure our self-worth by our long-term outcomes and the progress we make along the way.

Using Progress to Escape the Perfection Trap

Here's another truth about presenting a perfect image to the world: over time, it erodes your authenticity and sense of self. When you focus exclusively on perfection, you put yourself in a gruelling race against a world that is very mechanistic. But humans aren't robots. We can't perform at 100% all the time, nor should we try to.

Instead of focusing on the perfect outcomes, we need to focus instead on progress. Because that award you receive now will mean nothing in years to come. What you will remember, however, is the person you become on the route to receiving that award.

Measure the *progress* you make each day, week, month and year, rather than the *rewards* you receive along the way. This is about learning to enjoy the chase more than the kill. I'm not saying you shouldn't pause to celebrate those awards, you should. But also celebrate who you've become along the way. How you've adapted. What you've learnt.

Replace perfection with progress.

⊘ Mirror Time – *The Performance of Perfection*

? **Journal Prompt**

On a scale of 1 to 10, how driven are you by the need to "get it perfect"?

1 = Grounded, progress-focused, self-compassionate

10 = Driven, anxious, highly self-critical

Now ask yourself:

- What am I afraid people will think if I don't get it right?
- What would happen if I gave myself permission to be *messy*?
- What areas of my life am I stalling on because I'm afraid of being judged?

You don't need to be flawless to be free. You just need to be. . . enough. And you already are.

Act II, Scene 8

Make a Grudge List

"Who needs peace when you can keep score forever?"

[INT. WAREHOUSE – DOOR 8]

This door is heavier than the rest.

It's not locked, but you can feel the drag, as if it's carrying everything behind it.

Names are carved into the surface.

Some deep and jagged, others faint but still legible.

Some you recognise instantly.

Others make your chest tighten without knowing why.

The plaque reads:

"Ray – The Collector."

Future You rests a hand on the doorframe.

FUTURE YOU (low, steady):

"Every name here is a weight."

"Every weight is a wound."

"And every wound you refuse to clean. . . festers."

They nod once.

You push the door open.

🏚 Door 8 Opens: Meet Ray – The Collector

[INT. BASEMENT ROOM – LATE AFTERNOON]

The room smells of dust and paper.

Ray sits at a wooden table under a single bulb.

The light is dim, but you can see him writing in a large, leather-bound book.

Not a journal.

A **ledger**.

Pages filled with:

- Names.
- Dates.
- Specific offenses.
- The exact words said.
- The silence after.

Ray turns the page and adds another entry.

There's no rage in his face.

Just focus. Precision.

Like someone balancing accounts.

We flash through **years of ledgers** stacked in the corner:

- The friend who betrayed his trust.
- The boss who humiliated him.
- The sibling who borrowed and never returned.
- The partner who left without explanation.

Some are decades old.

None has faded.

In public, Ray laughs easily, shakes hands, plays the role.

But inside? The courtroom is always open.

And Ray is judge, jury, and warden.

◎ Dashboard Overlay – Door 8: Make a Grudge List

Metric	Status
Dopamine	● Minimal – no reward in replaying old pain.
Serotonin	▼ Suppressed – mood destabilised by unresolved resentment.
Cortisol	▲ Elevated – nervous system on permanent courtroom alert.
Oxytocin	▼ Blocked – trust restricted, connection filtered through suspicion.
Endorphins	▼ Inactive – no emotional release, tension stored.

Joy Meter

Status

■ Heavy – peace postponed, scorekeeping active.

[MONTAGE – HOW IT LIVES IN THE BODY]

- Shoulders permanently tense.
- Sleepless nights, replaying conversations from years ago.
- Heart rate spiking at the sight of a certain name.
- An acid taste in the mouth after thinking about "that thing" they did.
- Small joys interrupted by the sudden reappearance of old anger.

Ray doesn't realise it, but he's become an archivist of pain.

And the archive is killing him.

🎭 The Snap

A wedding invitation arrives in the mail.

It's from an old friend. Someone on the ledger.

Ray holds it. Turns it over in his hands.

He thinks about going.

He thinks about not going.

He thinks about what happened between them – for the thousandth time.

Finally, he drops the envelope in the bin.

But five minutes later. . . he takes it out again.

He doesn't open it.

Doesn't RSVP.

He just sits there, staring at it.

And whispers:

"Why does this still own me?"

[FADE TO BLACK]

🎬 **[INT. WAREHOUSE – BACK AT THE DOOR]**

You step out, and the weight follows you.

It's as if you've carried something back from that room.

Future You is watching you closely.

FUTURE YOU:

"You think grudges keep you safe."

"But they're not a shield."

"They're a shackle."

They step closer.

"Your brain doesn't know the difference between a fresh wound and a replayed one. Every time you revisit that moment, your body reacts as if it's happening now."

You frown. They go on.

"Those thoughts – they're not just floating ideas. They're physical structures in your brain."

"Neurons wiring together."

"Pathways getting stronger."

"Until the memory isn't just something you *have* – it's something you *are*."

They gesture towards the closed door.

"That's why you feel tired when you think about them. Why your joy drops without warning. You're not remembering – you're reliving. And your body is paying the price."

You feel it.

The low hum.

The silent vibration in your chest you've never been able to name.

Future You leans in.

"That hum you live with? It's not normal."

"That's the sound of joy suffocating."

"And the only way to kill it. . . is to let go."

You close your eyes.

You know exactly whose names are on *your* ledger.

💬 A Note from Jackson: The Silent Hum of Unforgiveness

I remember running a workshop once.

At the end, I gave everyone an assignment:

Write a letter of forgiveness to anyone who has wronged you.

The room went heavy.

You could feel the resistance in the air. It wasn't that they didn't understand forgiveness — they just didn't want to touch that locked drawer in their hearts.

But I knew:

Until you start the conversation of forgiveness, it doesn't happen.

I've seen firsthand how unforgiveness drains joy from your life.

When I first met my wife, she didn't have a good relationship with her father. Within weeks of knowing her, I told her something that made her look at me like I had two heads:

> *"You need to develop a better relationship with your dad. You need to forgive him and start loving again."*

I wasn't saying it to be insensitive. I said it because I knew I couldn't walk into a lifelong relationship with someone carrying that kind of bitterness toward a parent. We went on a journey together.

She chose to forgive. And the last years of her father's life were marked by reconciliation and joy. When he passed, yes, there was the bittersweet sting of wishing the reconciliation had happened sooner. But there was also the deep peace of knowing they didn't waste the time they had left.

The Truth About Forgiveness

Forgiveness isn't for the one who hurt you.

It's for **you**.

It's the release of venom from your bloodstream.

This isn't just a religious idea – although you'll find forgiveness at the heart of every major faith tradition. It's a *human* one.

Because life guarantees one thing: If you deal with people, you will be offended. If you collect every offense like it's an envelope handed to you on the street, soon you'll be walking around with a bag full of weighty, jagged-edged letters. By the time you get to the end of the road, you're limping. You can't move at the pace you want to.

That's what unforgiveness does.

It weighs you down – quietly, constantly.

Where your focus goes, your energy flows.

So, if your mind is preoccupied with an offence, that's where your focus will go. But more than that, your brain is an amplifier and a magnifier, which means the more you focus on grudges and offences, the more of those you see elsewhere in your life. Offences become bigger and louder.

This consumes you as a person and skews your perspective on life and happiness. Imagine you've only got 100GB of memory, but half of that is taken up by remembered offences. It won't be long before you're drained of storage and energy.

Holding grudges is like drinking poison and expecting the other person to die. The only one you're hurting is yourself.

We All Have a Grudge List

I can hear you about to deny it. But we do.

I do. You do. We all do.

When you put people on your grudge list, it's as though you're holding them hostage in the basement of your heart.

But here's the tricky part: Often you won't realise you're keeping them hostage. But if you didn't forgive them, they're down there. Along with that person who called you a name at primary school. And the clerk who spoke badly to you. And the person who cut you off on a roundabout on your drive to work yesterday.

You might not consciously think about them. But they're there. Each offence filed away by your subconscious. Each individual consigned to the basement of your heart.

So, the practice of unforgiveness is about sowing seeds in your subconscious mind to help release those hostages from the basement of your heart. Because you can't control your subconscious. But you can help direct it.

To do this you can physically write your grudge list.

Then for each name on your list, forgive them and physically check the name off the list.

This is how you can start to release those hostages you've been carrying for too long.

Writing a letter of forgiveness takes this a step further. Not everyone on your grudge list will require a letter. But the deeper the pain that person caused, the more important it is for you to write a letter of forgiveness. Express how the interaction affected you in order to be free of the offence.

Then thank the person you need to forgive for teaching you more about life.

Pause.

Keep thinking about the lessons you learnt from that scenario. As you focus on those lessons, the chemicals attached to the gift of the lessons will be released into your body.

I promise you'll feel lighter when you let them all go.

Practicing Advanced Forgiveness

Advanced forgiveness takes this process to the next level. It means that before I've even met you, I've chosen to forgive you because I accept that you're probably going to offend me. You are human, after all.

So, when anyone comes into my life, they have 49 tokens of forgiveness. Every time they offend me, I forgive them. That way, I don't let anyone else enter the basement of my heart.

I forgive quickly, because doing so keeps my heart and my mind lighter.

This practice also helps me approach others in this world with more grace and compassion.

You can also call it **positive paranoia**.

Whenever you feel yourself getting frustrated or angry with someone else, make up a story that's compassionate.

So, if I'm in a hurry when I'm driving and a woman two cars ahead of me starts slowing down for no reason I can see, I catch myself feeling frustration rising. Instead I make up a story about that woman that's more supportive. Maybe she's having a really bad day. She's a bit lost and is late for an appointment. My anger subsides. Instead I feel compassion.

I don't know if that story is true or not. But I'll never know either way. So I may as well create a story of compassion rather than one of offence.

🧠 The Science of Holding On

When something presents as a threat to your brain, it will loop it until it's no longer a threat. Here's an example: There's a spider in the corner of my bathroom which has been there for the last two weeks, posing a perceived threat. It hasn't got fangs. It's not going to bite me.

But there's a part of my brain that thinks, "Oh God, spiders will bite me."

The spider is still there because I'm too scared to move it. Because I think it will bite me.

But the spider isn't really the threat. The threat comes from the frame I've put around that spider. And my brain can't tell the difference.

Brain scans show that holding onto grudges and replaying offenses **activates the same neural circuits** as the original pain. Your brain doesn't know the difference between the memory and the moment; it experiences both as *now*.

Thoughts are not just ideas. They're **physical structures** in the brain. Neurons that fire together wire together, forming networks.

When you rehearse an offence, you strengthen the network of that memory. It becomes easier to access. . . and harder to escape.

Over time, these "unforgiveness circuits" link together, creating a mental *force field* that shapes how you interpret life. It keeps your nervous system in low-grade fight-or-flight mode, meaning cortisol stays elevated, heart rate variability stays poor, and your immune system is compromised.

Your joy isn't just an emotional casualty.

It's a **biological one**.

When your body becomes a pool of cortisol, it starts to damage your organs. You'll feel aches everywhere. This is when panic attacks kick in. And when you get ill more frequently, because your immune system is weak.

I once had a colleague who developed a lump on her wrist. When she went to see her doctor, she was told it was caused by stress. This is just one example of the very real physical consequences of elevated cortisol.

The Silent Hum

Here's the thing: Unforgiveness isn't in front of your face every day.

But it influences you every day.

It's like the low hum of a fridge – constant, almost invisible. You only notice it when it stops. When the fridge breaks and the sound is gone, you walk into the room and realise:

▌ *"Oh. This is what peace sounds like."*

When you think about people you love, it's a chorus of joy in your mind.

When you think about those you resent, it's that dark, ominous hum.

It's subtle, but it's always there – quietly poisoning the air you breathe.

Forgiveness is the switch that turns that hum off.

You don't forgive to make them right.

You forgive to make you *free*.

In some cases, like with my wife and her father, reconciliation is more appropriate than release. This is how you detox your heart and soul.

It's a daily exercise. Because you pick up crap every day, so you need to regularly purge your heart because you don't know how much weight you're carrying in your heart until you let it go.

How to Tell When You've Truly Forgiven

There will be certain people in our lives who hurt us more deeply than others. It can be hard to know when you've truly forgiven them.

The test I use is how you'd react if that person walked into the room right now. How do you feel? Is there still emotion there? Go as far as to imagine hugging them. If your first thought is "don't touch me," then you've still got some work to do.

Go back to the techniques I've shared. Write another letter of forgiveness. Thank them for the lessons. Focus on forgiveness.

⊘ Mirror Time – *The Silent Hum of Unforgiveness*

> ### ? Journal Prompt
>
> **On a scale of 1 to 10, how much of your mental and emotional space is occupied by unresolved offence?**
>
> *1 = Light, clear, emotionally free*
>
> *10 = Heavy, tense, constantly replaying past hurts*
>
> Now go deeper:
>
> - Whose names are still on your internal ledger? Write them down. Don't censor.
> - What exact moments or words still trigger a reaction in your body?
> - How long have you been carrying each one? Days? Months? Years?
> - What is it costing you to keep them? Energy? Relationships? Peace? Health?
> - What would your life feel like if you dropped even one name from that list today?
>
> You can't move freely if you're still carrying the weight.
>
> The pen you use to keep the list is the same pen that can cross out a name.

📖 Act II, Scene 9
Be Guided by Guilt

"Your moral compass runs exclusively on regret."

🎬 [INT. WAREHOUSE – DOOR 9]

This door isn't tall like the others.

You have to stoop to get through.

It forces you to bend before you've even entered – like it's training you to carry a weight.

The plaque reads:

▌ "Elias – The Weight Bearer."

Future You stands still for a moment before speaking.

FUTURE YOU (measured):

"If unforgiveness is a prison you build for others. . ."

"Guilt is the prison you build for yourself."

You both know it's time to go in.

🏠 Door 9 Opens: Meet Elias – The Weight Bearer

[INT. SMALL APARTMENT – EVENING]

Elias sits at the kitchen table.

The light is dim. His laptop is closed.

Bills on one side. A half-written letter on the other.

He picks up his pen. Writes a line.

Stops. Stares at it.

Sighs.

[MONTAGE – THE MENTAL REPLAY]

- The time he didn't make it to the hospital before his mother passed.
- The job offer he turned down that could have "changed everything."
- The relationship he walked away from without a word.
- The argument where he said too much – or not enough.
- The "if onlys" that keep him awake.

Elias is functional.

He goes to work. Smiles at the neighbours.

But inside? He's bent under the weight of every alternate version of his life that never happened.

Every decision is second-guessed.

Every moment is coloured by the thought:

"If I'd just done it differently. . ."

⚙ DASHBOARD OVERLAY

Metric	Status
Dopamine	▼ Starved – joy buried under regret load.
Serotonin	▼ Low – self-criticism erodes stability.
Cortisol	▲ Chronic high – constant stress replay.
Oxytocin	▼ Minimal – guilt isolates you from others.
Joy Meter	■ Almost empty – present moment hijacked.

🎭 The Snap

An email arrives from an old friend:

▌ *"Hey. Haven't heard from you in ages. Want to catch up?"*

Elias hovers over the reply button.

His heart races.

He whispers:

"I don't deserve to see them."

He closes the laptop.

Walks to bed.

And stares at the ceiling – still carrying the weight.

[FADE TO BLACK]

🎬 [INT. WAREHOUSE – BACK AT THE DOOR]

You step out and straighten your back, but you still feel it – the heaviness.

Future You looks straight at you.

FUTURE YOU:

"If forgiveness frees you from their offence. . ."

"Letting go of guilt frees you from *yours.*"

They keep going.

"Guilt can be useful when it's fresh – it's a compass, a signal to make things right. But if you let it calcify? It becomes cement in your soul."

They pause.

"The brain records guilt like it records trauma – and plays it back the same way."

"Each replay strengthens the neural loop."

"You're not just remembering the moment. . . you're reinforcing the belief that you can never outrun it."

"You can't rewrite the past."

"But you *can* rewire the future."

💬 A Note from Jackson: When Guilt Poisons the Moment

If unforgiveness is towards others, guilt is **self-directed unforgiveness**.

It's the regret of what you could have done.

Should have done.

Would have done – if only.

And here's the truth:

You can't go back.

You can only go forward.

But guilt tricks you into dragging the past into every room you enter.

It's the invisible boulder on your back, weighing down your words, your decisions, your joy.

Coming to Terms with My Own Guilt

For me, guilt took the shape of **unlived potential**.

Growing up, I had certain opportunities – especially in education – that I didn't fully maximise. At the time, I didn't see the cost. Years later, I realised it had stunted parts of my potential. That realisation? It turned into a dull, constant ache.

A whisper that said:

"If you'd done more, you'd *be* more."

Now, as a father, that ache sometimes turns into anxiety. I push my children to have every experience I missed. Every skill, every open door.

But here's the problem: That urgency doesn't always come from love – sometimes, it comes from **fear**.

And when guilt is driving, joy isn't in the car.

I feel guilty that I haven't necessarily been the dad my daughters need me to be.

I feel guilty that I haven't spent enough time with my parents. About whether I'm a good enough son, brother, and uncle. This is the guilt that lives in the background.

But this guilt isn't always grounded in reality. When I worry about whether I've missed years of my daughters' lives, I remind myself that one of them is five and the other is two. I haven't missed anything.

Then I focus on what actions I'm taking and will take to ensure I don't miss anything. Being present at bath time and play time. Being there when they need me at school. I focus on the action I'm taking to make our relationship better.

The Script in Your Brain

Sometimes you'll realise you should have done something. But instead of berating yourself for not doing it, recognise it and make sure you do it next time. That's healthy remorse.

I should have called my mother this evening. I didn't do it. I will do it tomorrow.

You're taking the regret, acknowledging it and taking positive steps to rectify it.

Toxic regret is when you focus on situations you can't change. Mistakes you've made that you can't fix. This is the regret that eats you up inside. Weighs heavy on your soul. Much like your grudge list.

If you are no longer able to physically do something about a situation, but you're still mulling it over, then it's toxic.

But don't feel bad if you uncover some toxic regrets running around your mind.

There's nothing wrong with *you*.

It's the script you're running. In your brain.

Neuroscience says:

Neurons that fire together, wire together.

Those old moments of guilt? They've fired so many times in your brain, they've wired together into a loop. Now that loop runs in the background, influencing your mood, shaping your choices, and stealing your joy without you realising.

To break free, you have to **unwire the loop and wire a new one**.

Later in this book, I'll give you the framework to do just that.

But for now, hear me:

Guilt doesn't serve you.

It will choke your joy.

And if left unchecked, it will corrode your soul.

Yes, this cuts deep – because it has to.

Because nothing changes until you see the damage for what it is.

You can't change the past.

But you *can* change what happens next.

⏀ Mirror Time – *The Weight You've Been Carrying*

❓ Journal Prompt

On a scale of 1 to 10, how much of your daily decision-making is influenced by guilt or regret?

1 = Free to act without regret pulling the strings

10 = Guided almost entirely by past mistakes

Now ask yourself:

- What memory am I still punishing myself for?
- What action have I avoided because I feel I "don't deserve" the outcome?
- If I forgave myself fully today, what would I do differently tomorrow?

Lighten the load.

Because joy walks faster without the boulder.

 Act II, Scene 10
Buy Personal Development Books and Don't Read Them

"Shelf-help > self-help."

▓ [INT. WAREHOUSE – DOOR 10]

This door is bright and cheerful.

Motivational stickers are plastered all over it:

- "Dream Big!"
- "Hustle Hard!"
- "Be the Best Version of You!"

The plaque reads:

▌ "Tara – The Librarian."

Future You smirks.

FUTURE YOU:

"Oh, you're going to recognise this one. You might even own half of what's in here."

They swing the door open.

🏛 Door 10 Opens: Meet Tara – The Librarian

[INT. LIVING ROOM – DAY]

It smells like ambition and fresh paper.

Books are everywhere; stacked on shelves, covering the coffee table, balanced on the floor in neat piles.

Sticky notes with online course logins are stuck to the fridge.

Browser tabs are filled with bookmarked webinar replays.

An unopened box sits in the corner, labelled: *"Masterclass Annual Membership Welcome Kit."*

Tara, wearing yoga pants and a "Level Up" hoodie, tears open a new Amazon delivery.

She breathes in the scent of a new book like it's her love language, then places it on the shelf – right next to 42 other unread titles.

⚙ DASHBOARD OVERLAY

Metric	Status
Dopamine	▲ Hit from buying, crash from not applying
Serotonin	● Temporary boost from "feeling prepared"
Cortisol	▲ Rises with guilt from inaction
Joy Meter	■ Looks engaged, feels stagnant

Tara calls herself a *lifelong learner*, but her learning is like Netflix browsing – thrilling until it requires commitment.

And sitting smugly in the corner, sipping coffee, is **Impostor Syndrome**.

🎭 IMPROV SCENE: Impostor Syndrome as Best Friend

IMPOSTOR SYNDROME:

"Great choice, Tara. This book is going to change everything."

TARA:

"Absolutely. I'll start it tomorrow."

IMPOSTOR SYNDROME:

"Sure, but first. . . maybe reorganise your shelves. And watch one more TED Talk. You know, to get in the right mindset."

Tara nods. They high-five.

Weeks pass.

Books gather dust.

Courses expire.

Ideas stay ideas.

Tara stays "busy" being prepared but never becomes equipped.

[FADE TO BLACK]

🎬 [INT. WAREHOUSE – BACK AT THE DOOR]

You step out with a smirk, but Future You's face is serious.

FUTURE YOU:

"Learning should be a bridge to action. But if you only collect the bricks, you'll never cross anywhere."

They tilt their head.

"Impostor Syndrome *loves* shelf-help. It keeps you feeling 'not ready' forever while looking busy enough to avoid the truth."

"You don't need more information. You need more implementation."

💬 A Note from Jackson

I've been in personal development for about 25 years.

I'm an avid reader – and a collector. A knowledge hoarder.

When I see a book, the cover, title, and subtitle pull me in like a tractor beam. They create a **flash of the future**; the promise that this will be the book that changes everything. That's not an accident. Book covers are designed to give you a dopamine hit before you've even turned a page.

It's the same rush some people get from buying shoes, handbags, or clothes. (And yes, my wife knows exactly what I mean – just in her own retail category.)

At my last count, I own around **1,700 books**.

Have I read them all? No.

Do I reference some? Yes.

Do I apply some? Definitely.

But the large majority? They just sit there, looking impressive, especially when I'm filming YouTube videos.

There's a Japanese word for this: **tsundoku** (積ん読).

It comes from:

- **tsunde** – to stack things
- **oku** – to leave for a while
- **doku** – to read

It means *"letting books pile up without reading them."*

Now, there's nothing wrong with collecting books – **if you're implementing them.**

The danger is when buying books becomes its own hobby. You feel productive, but it's really **intellectual procrastination.**

I know that I buy books under the delusion that the book I'm buying will solve the problem I have at the moment. But I often don't read beyond the first few pages. Then those books sit on a shelf. Gathering dust. A library of knowledge. Untapped.

The more I look at the books in my home, the more I see the challenge. And it comes from our friend dopamine again.

You see, when you buy a new book with the promise of a solution for a problem, your brain receives a shot of dopamine. Just like it does when you write a to-do list. That feels good. The shot of dopamine is what keeps us trapped in dopamine addiction cycles. This is where behaviour like Tara's stems from.

Knowledge Is. . .

Recently, on a webinar, I told the group: "Knowledge is. . ." and they shouted:

"Power!"

I said:

"No. Knowledge isn't power. Knowledge is prison – if you don't apply it."

When you hoard knowledge without action, you build an impressive, dopamine-rich prison. It feels good to wander its halls, but nothing changes.

The truth is, there's a massive gap between **what you know** and **what you do**.

That gap is where potential goes to die.

I'm guilty of it. I'll see a great title, buy it, imagine myself finishing it. . .and then it never happens. That fantasy doesn't develop me. It just gives me the *illusion* of growth.

So here's my new rule: **Act on it. Don't just collect it and stash it like a librarian of forgotten titles.**

A TikTok influencer gave me a tip I now swear by:

Every time you read a book, take one action per chapter.

Just one.

Not the whole thing at once.

That one action:

- Gives you a real sense of progress.
- Anchors the lesson in your brain.
- Triggers dopamine from *completion*, not just *purchase*.

That's how you beat tsundoku. You stop stacking. . . and start applying.

Read a Book Called *YOU*

Active implementation from books you've bought is good, but to take this one step further you need to stop reading other people's books and start reading a book called *YOU*. The only way to read that particular book is to take a long look in the mirror and ask yourself: "What needs to change?"

Look for long enough and you will get the answer. Once you have that answer, you can move to active implementation. And no, that's not an excuse to buy another book! Perhaps watch a video to help you solve the problem. Or see if the answer lies in a book you already own (and haven't read).

Sit with yourself and your thoughts before you take any action. Otherwise you might try to numb the pain you've uncovered from your self-reflection by putting another title on your shelf.

Many people find self-reflection uncomfortable. You feel vulnerable. But it's only by being vulnerable and opening up that you can get back to the core of who you are.

Finding Safety in Silence

It took time to feel safe in silence. At first, I felt deeply uncomfortable. But the more I made time to sit in silence, the more I started seeing the fruits of this practice. There was no music. No podcast. No TED Talks. No books. Just me and my thoughts.

And I realised this is how nature operates. The oak tree grows safe in silence, in the ground. It's just doing its thing. And I'm just doing mine.

Since I've embraced silence, I notice more. I hear more. I feel more. The results of my silence have become addictive and this has made silence a safe space for me instead of a deeply uncomfortable one.

⊘ Mirror Time – *Tsundoku &The Prison of Knowledge*

? Journal Prompt

On a scale of 1 to 10, how much of what you've learned in the last six months have you actually applied?

1 = Everything I consume, I act on

10 = Mostly collecting, barely applying

Now ask yourself:

- What's one book, course, or resource I've already bought that I can act on today?
- What's stopping me from implementing it?
- What's the smallest step I can take in the next 24 hours to apply it?

Your growth isn't in the pages.

It's in the practice.

 Act II, Scene 11
Compare Yourself to Everyone

"Especially that girl on LinkedIn with six job offers, a six-pack, and a six-figure side hustle. . . at six in the morning."

[INT. WAREHOUSE – DOOR 11]

The door is framed with mirrors. Big ones. Little ones. Warped ones. All of them labelled:

- "Boss Goals"
- "Body Goals"
- "Vacation Goals"
- "Why aren't YOU doing this yet?"

The plaque reads:

▌ **"James – The Approval Addict"**

Future You turns slowly to face you.

FUTURE YOU

"This is the most crowded room in the whole warehouse."

"Not because of how many people are in there. . ."

"But because of how many people live in your head."

The door opens.

🔐 Door 11 Opens: Meet James – The Approval Addict

[INT. MODERN FLAT – NIGHT]

James scrolls Instagram.

Then LinkedIn.

Then TikTok.

Then back to Instagram.

It's a loop.

Every swipe, a jab:

- One friend got promoted.
- Another launched a business.
- A third just announced their engagement and six-pack in the same post.

James sighs and clicks "like". . . again.

If comparison was a sport, James would have an Olympic gold, a podcast deal and a Netflix docuseries titled *"Me, Compared: The Story of Never Being Enough."*

[INT. KITCHEN – LATER THAT NIGHT]

James reheats leftovers. Stares into the microwave like it's judging him.

Voice in his head:

"You should've started that course."

"Look at your mate – already running a marathon."

"Why didn't you post your wins today? Do you even HAVE any?"

He picks up his phone again.

A post from a stranger: "Grind now. Shine later."

James sighs.

☼ DASHBOARD OVERLAY

Metric	Status
Dopamine	▲ Spiking from online validation.
Serotonin	▼ Low – joy tethered to external praise.
Cortisol	▲ High – mental overstimulation.
Oxytocin	▼ Absent – replaced by digital connection.
Joy Meter	◆ Critical – depends on likes & follows.

🎭 IMPROV SCENE: Comparison Crew Meeting

INSECURITY: "James, they're all better than you. Trust me."

FEAR: "Post that, and they'll laugh at you."

EGO: "Or. . . post something amazing and watch them love you. Again."

James hosts the meeting. . . every day.

[INT. BATHROOM – MIDNIGHT]

James brushes his teeth while watching a YouTube video: *"5 Habits of High Performers."*

He pauses.

Looks in the mirror.

But doesn't see himself.

Just. . . them.

All of them.

Everyone else.

[FADE TO BLACK]

[INT. WAREHOUSE – BACK AT THE DOOR]

You step out.

Future You is waiting with a hand mirror.

FUTURE YOU

"Comparison isn't just the thief of joy."

"It's the fraud of identity."

They pause.

FUTURE YOU (CONT'D)

"Comparison makes you perform instead of become."

"You chase applause instead of alignment."

They raise the mirror.

And this time, you see yourself – not the highlight reels.

Just you.

And somehow. . . that's enough.

💬 A Note from Jackson

I was running a staff training day once. Two hundred people in the room, all eyes forward.

I put up a slide that listed the "14 Costly Habits Killing Your Joy."

It didn't take long before the room got really honest.

A young lady sitting at the front raised her hand and said in front of *everyone:*

"I compare myself to other people all the time. Other professionals. People who are physically fit. People who seem to have it all together. And it really frustrates me."

From another table, someone called out:

"It's all a lie!"

And she was right.

I backed her up.

"Yes. It's all a lie. Because we're lying to ourselves – about the *whole* truth."

The Cost of Lying to Yourself

The most dangerous person in the world to lie to is yourself. We all know that the impact of lying to others is destroying relationships. But when you lie to yourself, your brain no longer trusts you. In doing so, you're **destroying your relationship with yourself**.

That saps your strength.

It weakens you. It weakens your ability. It weakens your resolve.

And it affects your self-esteem. Because if you constantly lie to yourself, you won't see yourself as a valuable person.

That's just further fuel for comparison. You devalue yourself *internally* and then you compare yourself to what you see in others *externally*.

So, What Is the *Whole* Truth?

We don't know what's going on in other people's heads.

We don't know the pressure behind their performance, the tears behind their TikToks, the tension in their relationships, or the skeletons in their digital closets.

That's why this quote hit me hard when I first heard it:

> **"Never compare someone else's outside with your inside."**

Every other creation on this planet reaches its full potential without comparison. Trees don't compare bark textures. Birds don't envy each other's wing spans. A sunflower doesn't look at a daisy and say, "Ugh. Must be nice to be short and cute."

They just *grow*.

They just obey the code written inside them.

But us? We override ourselves.

Because of our awareness.

Because of our brains.

Because we scroll when we're low. And compare when we're tired.

If this sounds familiar. . . you're not alone.

But the truth remains:

You are not behind.

You are not broken.

You are not them – and that's exactly your superpower.

Your job is not to keep up.

Your job is to keep going as *you*.

But why does that feel so hard?

Think about this for a moment. Throughout your entire life, you watch other people succeed. You see them because you are outward facing. But the one person you don't see is *yourself.* This is crucial. Because your brain is always processing what it sees. But your eyes never roll inward to see who you are. So you automatically take what you see on the outside of everyone else, feel empty and start comparing.

Over the years I've noticed how comparing myself to others created the wrong competitive drive. It ties back to mimetic desire, which we discussed earlier, and how you can end up chasing goals and dreams that aren't even yours.

Comparison strengthens that.

It feeds it.

But you need to stop looking at others and start looking inwards. That's easier said than done, especially in the modern world, because the more accessible the world is, the more fuel you have for your comparison fire.

This is why sitting in silence is so valuable. Pulling away from the world for a few moments can allow you to tune in internally and come back to who you really are.

Seeing Yourself for Who You Are

There is an exercise I carried out that was very helpful for helping me build a truer perception of myself. It might sound counterintuitive, because I'm going to tell you to ask other people what they think of you, but roll with it.

Here's the task:

Send a message to a group of people in your life who you trust and ask them to give you three words that they would use to describe you.

When I asked for three words that people in my circle would use to describe Jackson, the answers I received were very consistent. They reinforced what I already knew about myself and helped me be more intentional going forward.

Trust this process.

You might receive answers you don't want to hear. But if 15 people all say the same thing you don't like, that's a hard mirror that you need to stare into.

When you're choosing people to ask, make sure they're qualified for the role. By which I mean:

- You've spent enough time with them.
- You love them and they love you.
- You trust them.
- They've seen you in all the seasons of your life.

That's it. Those are the qualifications.

I know this exercise can be scary. It is revealing. Vulnerable. But when you do it you strip away your mask. And in doing so what you discover will be liberating.

Stopping the Scroll

We can't talk about comparison without acknowledging the role that social media plays in our lives. The algorithms on these platforms are designed to learn your interests and feed those back to you.

Unlike the trusted people you reach out to for the exercise I just shared, the algorithm doesn't care about you. It doesn't want your money, or your time. It wants your soul. That might sound dramatic, but here's why:

Because once it has your soul, it has your time, attention, and money.

Your soul in this context is your intellect, emotions and will. That last one – **your will** – is crucial, because once you surrender your will, that algorithm owns you and your choices.

The sad part is that the majority of people know they're addicted to the algorithm. But you need to consciously increase your awareness about it. Wilful ignorance is the worst choice in this scenario.

I remember watching the documentary *Social Media Dilemma* and being so shocked by what I learnt that I gave up my smartphone for 76 days.

That helped me get back to centre.

Am I perfect? No.

Do I still find myself scrolling sometimes? Yes.

The golden rule if you do slip into the cycle of scrolling again is **no guilt**.

Be proud that you caught yourself in the act. Put your phone aside. Forgive yourself and move on.

Remember our addiction to scrolling on social media comes from dopamine. But every time we get cheap dopamine hits, we're just raising our tolerance to its effects. Which means we need more of it to get the same impact in future.

The counterbalance to this addiction?

Gratitude and joy.

When you have gratitude and joy, you dramatically reduce the dopamine craving that you're chasing. By reminding yourself what you have, you put yourself in a state of fullness rather than a state of lack. All of a sudden, what you see on your feed doesn't feel as appealing. Because you have what you need. Right here.

Earlier in this book I told you about my meditation spot with a tree.

While I was writing this chapter, I went up there. It's the end of autumn. The tree is shedding its leaves. Getting naked. Preparing for winter. It's beautiful.

That gratitude for nature helps me appreciate what season of my life I'm in. Sometimes I'll go through a seasonal transition too. My leaves will fall, and I'll be stripped bare. But my roots are still grounded.

Fill Up with Gratitude

The exercise I'm about to share with you will take about an hour of your time, but it will keep you fulfilled with gratitude for three months.

You're going to make a list of 100 things you're grateful for in different categories of your life.

Write down:

- Everything you've achieved.
- What you've bought, why you bought it, and when.
- Places you've visited.
- Where you live.
- People you love.
- Experiences you've had.

Next to each thing that you put on your list, write **why it is important**.

Making a list like this makes you feel full emotionally. It fills your heart and your mind.

◎ Mirror Time – The Trap of Measuring Your Life with Someone Else's Ruler

---

> ### ❓ Journal Prompt
>
> *On a scale of 1 to 10, how often do you find yourself comparing your life to others (online or offline)?*
>
> *1 = I stay in my lane and clap for others genuinely*
>
> *10 = I can't scroll for five minutes without spiralling*

 Act II, Scene 12
Complain About Everything

"Solutions are overrated when whining is an option."

[INT. WAREHOUSE – DOOR 12]

This door is creaking. . . loudly.

It groans with every gust of air, as if even it has something to say about its condition.

The plaque reads:

▌ **"Gavin – The Professional Whiner"**

Future You raises an eyebrow.

FUTURE YOU:

"This one's fun. . . until it isn't."

They open the door with a sigh.

A very dramatic sigh.

Because obviously, everything is just *so hard*.

🏠 Door 12 Opens: Meet Gavin – The Professional Whiner

[INT. OPEN-PLAN OFFICE – DAY]

The camera pans across an office filled with chatter, keyboard clicks, and the smell of microwaved lunches.

We zoom in on a desk with a "World's Okayest Employee" mug.

Meet Gavin.

He's already mid-rant.

GAVIN:

"The traffic was horrendous. The weather's a joke. This coffee is luke-warm. My manager? Clueless. My team? Useless. And don't even get me started on the new diversity training. . ."

A colleague walks by.

COLLEAGUE:

"Morning Gavin!"

GAVIN:

"Is it?"

🖥 GAVIN'S DESKTOP:

Tabs open:

- "Why am I always tired?"
- "Workplace stress symptoms"
- "Top 10 signs you're surrounded by idiots"

⚙ DASHBOARD OVERLAY

Metric	Status
Dopamine	▼ Drained – reward system overloaded by negativity.
Serotonin	▼ Minimal – no gratitude input.
Oxytocin	▼ None – relational bonds weakened by pessimism.
Endorphins	▼ Dormant – no movement, no joy.
Cortisol	▲ HIGH – chronic stress loop.
Joy Meter	■ Critically low – empathy exhaustion in progress.

🎭 COMEDY SKETCH: "The Complain Games™"

The camera cuts to a mock Olympic arena.

ANNOUNCER (V.O.):

"Welcome to the Complain Games – where nobody wins and everybody whines!"

- Gavin takes gold in "Microwave Moaning"
- Silver in "Passive-Aggressive Emails"
- Bronze in "Eye Rolls per Minute"

A reporter asks Gavin if he's happy with his medals.

GAVIN:

"They could've been shinier."

🎬 The Snap

Back in the office. Gavin stares at the screen.

Slack pings.

He groans.

Email pings.

He groans louder.

Phone rings.

He lets it go to voicemail.

Suddenly. . . he glances at the window.

A team across the street is outside doing yoga. Laughing. Moving. Living.

He watches.

His hand slowly moves to his phone.

Then puts it down.

Opens his email.

Finds a draft he never sent titled:

▌ **"My Resignation Letter."**

He deletes it.

Sighs. Again.

[FADE TO BLACK]

🎬 **[INT. WAREHOUSE – BACK AT THE DOOR]**

You step out and Future You hands you a tissue.

FUTURE YOU:

"Complaining is addictive."

"It feels like release. But it's just resistance dressed in drama."

They turn to you:

"When you repeat the problem, your brain thinks you're solving it. But you're not."

"You're just training yourself to stay stuck."

They gesture towards the next door.

FUTURE YOU:

"The opposite of complaining isn't silence."

"It's ownership."

💬 **A Note from Jackson**

I remember once running a leadership training session and asking everyone to list what they'd complained about that week. It was silent for a bit until one person started.

And then? The floodgates opened.

From packed trains to printer jams, to politics and partners. It was a joy massacre.

But here's the thing:

I wasn't judging them.

Because I saw myself in all of them.

Complaining is easy. Addictive. Socially acceptable. It gives us a false sense of community.

You complain, I nod. I complain, you nod. We bond over our mutual misery. But what are we building?

Nothing.

Just echo chambers of unprocessed pain.

But this deep human need for community and connection encourages us to keep complaining. Especially when those around us share their own complaints back to us. Mutual complaining creates rapport and a false sense of security.

It took me years to realise that *complaining isn't about the thing*. It's about the state of the soul.

When you're joyful, solutions excite you.

When you're low? Complaints are comfort food.

I'm not saying never speak your truth. But know when it's a rant and when it's a request.

One leads to freedom.

The other just feeds frustration.

We all need to vent sometimes. That's human. It's how we get back to balance, by letting out what's troubling us. The problems come when you get addicted to complaining. When you see this as your best route to security.

It's a loop that can be easy to get stuck in.

Breaking the Complain Loop

Without wishing to sound like a superhero, I have trained myself not to complain. If I sense a complaint about to come out of myself, I literally stop myself talking. I have done this because I know that complaining is dangerous. So I put myself in gratitude mode.

You can do it too. It takes practice, but once you get it, you'll feel complaints die before they have a chance to surface.

Picture the scene:

I'm sitting at a desk piled with letters that I've been avoiding dealing with.

My mind starts to think *Oh my gosh. Look at all these letters. . .* The second I catch myself about to complain about those letters, I flip my perspective. I give thanks for having the opportunity to deal with the letters. I visualise what I'm going to get on the other side of having gone through the letters. And I get on with it.

Gratitude. Reward. Action.

It's a simple system, but it works.

Words Matter

The words we use matter, whether we're saying them to someone else or to ourselves. This doesn't only apply in relation to complaining. You'll notice intentional words are a theme throughout this book.

Here's an alternative script I teach to children: "When I complain it affects my brain."

Say that a few times in a human, humorous way and you'll find you stop complaining. You feel silly saying it. Which helps you see the absurdity of your complaint.

Another one to try if you're slipping into self-pity is: "Feeling sorry for myself won't help myself."

Say it over and over again. Remind your brain that there is another option.

Words matter so much that there are certain words that are banned in my family. Top of the list is "difficult."

Why? Because the second you use that word you'll be stressed for a week. Instead we use the word "adventurous."

Earlier this week, I was taking my daughter to school. Her younger sister was along for the ride, strapped into her car seat. As I pulled away from our house, I got a whiff of something funny.

Unpleasant.

Pungent.

I wound down the window, wondering if my youngest needs a nappy change. But no.

The smell is persistent.

And it's coming from the front of the car.

I looked down. There was the culprit.

My older daughter had stepped in dog poo.

I turned around and headed home to deal with the smelly shoe. I wash it as fast as I can, put it back on her foot. Now we're ten minutes late.

I can still smell it everywhere in the car, but I decide we just need to get her to school.

That's when she pipes up:

"Oh, that was adventurous!"

All of a sudden, that problematic situation was framed as an adventure.

Imagine how much better and more joyful your days would be if they were filled with **adventurous moments** instead of difficult moments?

There's a reason we use the phrase: "I had to laugh or I'd cry. . ."

Turn frustrating to **funny**.

Anxious to **adventurous**.

Tired to **in need of an energy top-up**.

When someone asks how you are, swap "not bad" for:

"Amazing."

"Wonderful."

"Things are superb."

Notice how it makes you feel.

⊘ Mirror Time – *Emotional Echo Chambers*

> **? Journal Prompt**
>
> *On a scale of 1 to 10, how much of your day is spent repeating what's wrong. . . vs. resolving it?*
>
> *1 = Solution-driven and energised*
>
> *10 = Certified moaner with a PhD in pessimism*

 Act II, Scene 13
Avoid Delegation at All Costs

"Trust issues build character. . . or something."

📽 **[INT. WAREHOUSE – DOOR 13]**

This door is covered in *Post-it notes.*

Some say "REMEMBER," others just say "ME."

There's a faint smell of burnt toast and burnout.

The plaque reads:

▌ **"Melissa – The Martyr Manager"**

Future You folds their arms.

FUTURE YOU:

"Here lies the shrine of control."

"Built brick by brick. . . out of trust issues."

They hand you a clipboard before opening the door.

🏠 Door 13 Opens: Meet Melissa – The Martyr Manager

[INT. HOME OFFICE – EVENING]

Melissa is juggling three things at once.

- She's on Zoom – smiling.
- She's WhatsApping her friend – "Can't talk. Chaos. x"
- She's also cooking dinner.

(Something is smoking. It's probably the chicken. . . or her brain.)

Her partner pops their head in:

PARTNER:

"Need help with anything?"

MELISSA (snapping):

"No, it's fine. I've got it."

But she doesn't "got it."

Her email inbox is a war zone.

The birthday cupcakes for her kid's school are still raw in the middle.

She hasn't peed since 9 a.m.

⚙ DASHBOARD OVERLAY

Metric	Status
Dopamine	● Short spikes from task-ticking. . . followed by dread.
Serotonin	▼ Low – no social bonding or rest to lift mood.
Oxytocin	▼ Drained – isolation from refusing support.
Endorphins	▼ Flatline – no release, no rest, no reward.
Cortisol	▼ HIGH – chronic overload, micro-traumas stacking.
Joy Meter	■ Warning: Operating in martyr mode.

🎭 SATIRE INTERLUDE: "The Delegation Circus Show"

ANNOUNCER (V.O.):

"Welcome to the Delegation Circus Show! Today's featured act: **Doing Everything Yourself While Resenting Everyone Who Doesn't Help!**"

Melissa appears in the ring.

First, she sprints around the ring, balancing ten plates on sticks and keeping them all spinning. When the first plate hits the ground with a crash, the lights go out.

Spotlight on.

Melissa is back. This time carrying the weight of her mental load. She's like a strongman of days gone by, lifting the barbell over her head. The dull thud as she drops it signals another costume change.

Now Melissa is in a leotard, contorting herself into weird and wonderful shapes as she performs her silent suffering gymnastics routine.

Audience rating: 10/10 for internal resentment. 0/10 for actual help received.

🎬 The Snap

Melissa finally collapses on the couch.

Her child walks in holding a half-burnt cupcake.

CHILD:

"Mummy, you forgot the birthday note."

Melissa stares at the cupcake.

Burnt on the outside.

Raw on the inside.

Just like her.

She forces a smile.

But one tear escapes.

Not because of the cupcake.

Because she's tired of being a one-woman army with no medals.

[FADE TO BLACK]

🎬 [INT. WAREHOUSE – BACK AT THE DOOR]

You step out, winded.

Future You is already scribbling something on the clipboard.

FUTURE YOU:

"There's a cost to doing it all yourself."

"And it's not just exhaustion – it's disconnection."

They circle one word on the clipboard:

"TRUST."

FUTURE YOU:

"Refusing to delegate isn't heroic."

"It's just fear in a fancier outfit."

They point to the next door.

"You want your joy back?"

"Start letting go."

💬 A Note from Jackson

I used to think that doing everything myself was a badge of honour.

Truth is, it was just trauma wearing a to-do list.

Delegation scared me.

Why?

Because deep down, I didn't trust that anyone could do it *my* way.

I didn't trust that letting go wouldn't mean letting down.

Until I hit a wall.

Burnout.

Bitterness.

Boredom from trying to be brilliant at everything.

Here's what I've learned:

- Delegation isn't about dumping tasks.
- It's about sharing **trust** and **growth**.
- It's not weakness.
- It's *wisdom*.

Now?

I let go faster.

I train better.

And I don't wait until the tears come to realise: **Help is holy.**

But let's rewind a bit. I spent 15 years running a business where I should have delegated more. If I had, my business would likely be running in multiple places around the world now. Instead, I built around me to feel good about myself. And to build something that felt good, I thought I needed to control everything.

I lost sight of my mission. I wasn't trying to build something that would help the world. I was building for self-validation.

This is where so many high achievers lose sight of what's important. So ask yourself, why are you high achieving in the first place? To change the world or to validate yourself?

If it's the former, you have to let go. Because you will **go further and faster when you're not alone**.

Here's where the magic lies.

Since I relinquished control over everything, I have more time, more peace and more ideas. I'm empowering more people, which in turn helps me feel more centred.

Because it's not about me.

The Heavy Loads We All Carry

There are two questions we all carry around with us subconsciously. They're like millstones around our necks:

- Am I enough?
- Am I loved?

The way those loads manifest is different for all of us in different areas of our lives. Whether in relation to business, parenting, family, friendship. But if you don't feel loved or you don't feel enough, you turn to what you can do practically to change it.

You start coming up with ideas. Firing off emails. Writing to-do lists.

Overwhelm hits.

It's like you've got 15 PAs all running at you with questions and bits of paper in their hands. You can't answer them all at once. So you hide in the broom cupboard.

A Framework for Delegation

If you recognise that you need to delegate, first zoom out and look at the big picture. What are you trying to achieve? Once you have the end in mind you can work backwards to delegate the tasks you need help with to make your impact.

When you're delegating, you simply have to remember the three Ts.

- Time
- Training
- Trust

The more time you spend with someone, the more trained they will be and the more trustworthy they become. However, you need to be realistic. They are unlikely to achieve a level 10, your level, in the task you're delegating. They might stick at level seven. And you have to accept that seven. Embrace it even. Because at the same time, they will be mastering things that you are rubbish at. And that is what will support you to become great at what *you* are great at.

But you also have to accept there will be some things that only you can do.

According to Pareto's Principle, only 20% of what you do in life you have to do, but 80% of what you do can be delegated. Cleaning your house can be delegated. So can cooking. Even shopping. You might not be able to afford to delegate all those tasks, but they are delegatable.

Loving my wife and children can't be delegated to someone else though. Neither can loving my family and friends.

When you are deciding what to delegate, ask yourself:

"If somebody else did this, would it take anything away from me as a person?"

Then ask:

"Am I the only person qualified to do this task?"

Then:

"Really? Am I really the only person qualified to do this task?"

Then:

"Am I really, really the only person qualified to do this task?"

If you're still saying "Yes" to that third layer of the question, you know it's a task you can't delegate.

Keep a lookout for any signs that you're sliding back into martyr mode. Stress. Burnout. Tiredness. Irritability. Overwhelm. A lack of appreciation for the small things in life. Maybe food doesn't taste as rich. Or that song you love no longer makes you spark. Watch for these signs you're becoming numb towards life. And take action to delegate so you can return to yourself.

Help Is Holy

One of the biggest stumbling blocks in relation to delegation is often the act of asking for help in the first place.

But throughout your life, you are being helped every day.

You didn't build the house you live in. You didn't build your car. When you slept last night, you did not filter your liver. You did not keep your heart functioning. Something is helping you, so why not consciously accept help in business and in life too?

I'm serious. Look around you. Help is everywhere. You exist because you are being helped, so lean into that.

The safety, security, and success you feel in life exists because someone helped you. Duplicate it. Remodel it.

My faith has helped me embrace the concept of asking for help, because I always feel supported. I know that when I do wrong, God has my back. When I'm lost, they'll find me. And knowing that has put me in a position where I can help others seek that same security.

But make no mistake, there is a cultural narrative around asking for help that needs to shift. The news we read, watch, and listen to every day is filled with negativity. Asking for help is portrayed as a sign of weakness.

It's not.

It's strength.

It's a sign you know yourself.

That you know you can go further when you travel together.

◈ Mirror Time – *The Prison of Perfectionism & Control*

❓ Journal Prompt

On a scale of 1 to 10, how much are you currently carrying alone that could be shared?

1 = Delegating like a boss
10 = Martyr mode: full activation

📖 Act II, Scene 14
Glorify Busyness

"Because if you're not drowning in stress, are you even living?"

🎬 [INT. WAREHOUSE – DOOR 14]

This door hums.

Not a sweet melody.

It hums like a machine. A factory.

Always on. Always producing. Always spinning.

The plaque reads:

▌ **"Denise – The Hustle Queen"**

Future You sighs.

FUTURE YOU (dryly):

"Brace yourself. This one wears exhaustion like a badge of honour."

You nod.

You already know.

You've felt it.

They open the door.

🏠 Door 14 Opens: Meet Denise – The Hustle Queen

[INT. OPEN PLAN OFFICE – NIGHT]

There she is.

Denise.

Still at her desk.

Everyone else has gone home.

She's replying to emails with one hand, eating a cold Pret sandwich with the other.

There's a notification on her phone.

Another "Mindfulness Tip of the Day" ping.

She ignores it.

Again.

Denise doesn't *slow down*.

She *can't*.

She's booked back-to-back meetings with no buffer.

Her inbox has more flags than the United Nations.

And yet. . . she's volunteering to run the bake sale on Saturday.

Because, of course.

She's *needed.*

She's *important.*

She's the glue.

The engine.

The one who never stops.

Until. . . she does.

☼ DASHBOARD OVERLAY

Metric	Status
Dopamine	⬤ Short spikes, followed by crashes.
Serotonin	▼ Dropping – no time for self-worth.
Cortisol	▼ HIGH – long-term overload.
Oxytocin	▼ Distant – no time for connection.
Joy Meter	■ Red Zone – danger of burnout.

🎭 SATIRICAL INTERLUDE: THE BUSYNESS OSCARS

🎤 HOST:

"We're here to celebrate those who seem to do the most at the Busyness Oscars!"

They pull out a gleaming gold envelope.

"And the winner of Best Busyness Actor is. . . Denise! For her role *Crying silently in the shower while mentally rehearsing a Zoom presentation.*"

"Next we have Best Supporting Busyness Actor. . ."

Another gold envelope.

"And the winner is. . . Denise! For her role in *One-handed spreadsheet management while stirring dinner.*"

🎬 [INT. HOME – LATE NIGHT]

Denise finally gets home.

Her kids are asleep.

She missed bath time. Again.

She stares at herself in the bathroom mirror.

Hair falling out of its updo.

Eyes tired.

Heart. . . heavier than usual.

She whispers:

"I'm doing all this. . . for them."

But the reflection whispers back:

"Are you though?"

[FADE TO BLACK]

🎬 [INT. WAREHOUSE – BACK AT THE DOOR]

Future You turns to you.

FUTURE YOU:

"Denise never set out to burn herself out."

"She just thought busy meant valuable."

"But when your worth is tied to your workload. . . you'll always feel bankrupt."

They pause.

FUTURE YOU:

"Busyness is not a badge."

"It's a blindfold."

You take a breath.

And suddenly, you feel how fast your own life has been spinning.

💬 A Note from Jackson

I remember being in a school, giving a talk on exam pressure. A student raised their hand and said:

"Sir, if I'm not busy, I feel guilty."

Whew.

That hit.

And I said:

"Feeling guilty for resting is a system failure. You've been programmed to overwork. But you're not a machine."

We've normalised the grind.

Worshipped the hustle.

Sacrificed joy at the altar of performance.

But joy isn't found in the busyness.

It's found in being present.

So if you've been busy chasing everything. . . maybe it's time to pause and ask if joy's been chasing you – but you were too busy to notice.

Acceleration Without Accomplishment

When you wear "busy" like a badge of honour, you're not actually going anywhere. There might appear to be acceleration. But without accomplishment, what's the point?

For our brains, dopamine is the point. We get a dopamine hit from being busy. And we're so busy chasing the next fix, we don't stop to question whether the activities we're so busy with are authentic.

The next time you feel yourself being "busy," pause. Ask: "Is this a dopamine fix or is this me being necessarily busy?"

I've spent time caught in a whirlpool of busyness. Aimlessly spinning but never going anywhere. It made me ineffective. Which has affected my progress in business. Which has affected my profits and progress in life. Which has affected my mental health. That caused me to pause. To come back to myself. To examine my "busyness."

I felt it in the disconnection from my wife. In the distance from my girls.

Now, if I have a few weeks of busyness, where I'm necessarily travelling a lot, I balance it with two weeks spent with my family.

What Are You Running From?

When you are constantly busy, it is usually because you are running from the truth. Busyness can be a mask. It can be medication and numb you to the truth. And that's what makes it so dangerous.

During my pause, I faced my truth. I pictured myself going down Anxiety Avenue, which can lead to Depression Boulevard. I was able to sense my potential trajectory. And that scared me. I've heard too many horror stories – the seemingly happiest of people taking their own lives – and I did not want to become one.

The second you get the signals, pay attention.

My big pause has caused me to become more balanced, more aware, more in tune, more grateful and, initially, more anxious. But that anxiety has now given way to excitement. **I want to live here now.**

I've reached a place of spiritual stillness, after having lost myself in the physical and mental planes. Pausing allowed me to reconnect with my true identity in the spiritual realm. That stillness has made me more productive back in the physical world, because I'm now going into activities a lot more grounded.

I no longer determine whether I've had a productive day based on how many tasks I did or didn't complete. For me, a productive day is one where I've gone with the flow and allowed the day to be what it is.

Perhaps the most important thing to remember is that we are all going to die one day. You can either speed it up or slow it down.

By resting.

Rest slows atrophy, because when you rest, you're not over using your organs. And you're giving them time to recover.

Also remember that the busyness you carry will simply pass to someone else at some point. If you left your job today, your company would hand off all your "busyness" to other people in the blink of an eye.

So the lesson is **please put yourself first**.

Normalise rest. Shut down over your lunch break. Log off in the evening. Sleep well.

⌀ **Mirror Time – The Cult of Hustle**

? Journal Prompt

On a scale of 1 to 10, how glorified is "being busy" in your life?

1 = I honour rest, boundaries, and presence
10 = If I stop moving, I panic

Now ask yourself:

- What *real* emotions am I avoiding by staying constantly busy?
- What's one thing I can say "no" to this week without the world falling apart?
- If I stopped equating busyness with worth. . . what would change?

Thank you for getting to the end of Act 2. As a thank you, I would love for you to meet some of the characters in the 14 doors, so we have something special for you. Visit www.JacksonOgunyemi.com to see what it is.

 # Act III
The Shift

Pause now to absorb what you've learnt by walking through those 14 doors. Call this the interval if you will, before we dive into Act III.

We've just been on a deep journey to the heart of human happiness.

Here is the truth that I want you to grasp at this point:

This process is more than self-improvement.

It is rewiring.

Think of it as a fundamental upgrade to your own personal "app." Each time you address one of these costly behaviours, you are coding your app, the default that lies at the heart of who you are. The app that drives your identity. When you build the behaviours for joy and happiness into the heart of your app, you stop having to build new habits. You stop having to try to change.

Instead, those behaviours become built in.

Part of your default way of being.

Sometimes the noise of the world can mean you lose sight of your default. But it's always there. In the silence. The stillness. All you have to do is reset.

Even on the busiest of days, I can find my silence, my stillness. I use this phrase as a reminder when I need it:

Be in the storm, but don't let the storm be in you.

This is about focusing on how you move through the world. Not about how many new habits you can build into your life.

When you build your app to this default standard, it will trigger naturally. A mistake I made in the past was trying to build habits faster and better. The shift came when I stopped building habits and started building my identity. The person I want to be.

This is not a fad. Or a life hack. This is **how you become**.

Become who you truly are.

Become who you are meant to be.

And once you become, the app will do the work for you.

This is deep work. But this book that you hold in your hands is your guide. And when you feel this work is too heavy, just say these words to yourself:

> **"I am now a new person. I am working on who I want to become."**

So, let's return to the warehouse to see the process of becoming. To better understand how you can build your app and create a default operating system that brings more joy and happiness into your life.

Act III, Scene 1
The Aftermath
in the Warehouse

[INT. WAREHOUSE – BACK IN THE MAIN ROOM]

The last door has closed.

You're standing in the centre of the warehouse again.

Still.

Quiet.

A little stunned.

You've just walked through 14 doors.

Each one punched, poked and whispered something you've been avoiding.

Behind you, each door pulses faintly like a heartbeat you can't ignore.

Future You stands across from you.

Arms crossed.

161

Gentle smile.

Waiting.

Then finally, they speak.

🧠 FUTURE YOU (MONOLOGUE)

"You're not broken."

"You're just. . . *repeating*."

"Mirrors don't show your reflection."

"They show your *repetition*."

"That was never meant to shame you; it was meant to wake you."

"Do you know how rare that is?"

"To actually wake up to yourself?"

"Most people sleepwalk through their lives. Eyes open, hearts closed."

"They feel something is wrong, but they can't quite name it."

"You just named it 14 times."

"And the beautiful part?"

"Once you name it, you can change it."

"Awareness isn't guilt."

"Awareness is *freedom* knocking on your door."

"I didn't bring you here to hurt you."

"I brought you here to *help* you."

"I've walked both timelines – the joyful one, and the one where you kept postponing your happiness."

"I know what it's like to ache with regret."

"I know what it's like to finally breathe with freedom."

"This moment? Right now? This is your *choice point*."

(They gesture around the warehouse.)

"So. Tell me. . ."

"Which of the 14 hit you hardest?"

"Which ones whispered, 'That's me'?"

"Be honest with yourself. Write them down. Own them. Don't just nod. Name them."

(They pause, watching you).

"And how are you feeling?"

"Truly. Underneath it all."

"Are you angry? Numb? Liberated? Grateful? Confused? Inspired? It's all valid."

(Beat).

"So what now?"

"You've admitted. Reflected."

"Now what do you do?"

You look at them.

They smile.

Big.

Warm.

Borderline smug.

YOU:

"Why are you smiling?"

FUTURE YOU:

"Because. . . that's the answer."

YOU:

"What? Just. . . smile?"

FUTURE YOU:

"Yes. You need to SMILE."

You're still looking at Future You.

Still reeling.

Still unsure how a simple smile could be the solution.

They lean forward with a grin and say:

FUTURE YOU:

"Let me tell you a dream I had once."

"It might help this all make sense. . ."

☾ THE DREAM SEQUENCE BEGINS

"The Morning I Woke Up Inside My Mind"

An Allegory of the SMILE Framework

(Self-Reflection, Mastery, Implementation, Liberation, Environment)

It started like any regular morning –

Except one major red flag.

I opened my eyes and above me, staring back, was a **massive mirror** covering my entire ceiling.

Yes. A mirror.

I blinked twice. It was still there.

I turned over – mirrors on the walls too.

The hallway? Mirrors.

The bathroom? Mirrors.

I couldn't escape my reflection if I tried.

There I was:

Sleep-crusted eyes. Gravity-defying bed hair.

And a startled look that screamed:

"What is happening to my life?"

So naturally, I jumped out of bed.

And, as one does when surrounded by ceiling-mounted surveillance mirrors, I grabbed my **Samurai sword**.

(. . .Don't ask why there's a Samurai sword in my house. Just stay with me.)

Now holding this weapon of precision and ancient honour, I crept through my mirror maze of a home.

Nerves shot. Adrenaline high.

And then it happened.

BANG.

I tripped.

Over a **10-ft hammer** lying right in the middle of the hallway.

At this point, my toe was throbbing.

My sword was spinning across the floor like a flying boomerang.

And my morning was shaping up to be a full-blown *psychological thriller*.

I screamed. Because of course.

So I did what any semi-rational person would do:

I ran outside.

And that's when salvation arrived in the most bizarre, Disney-meets-therapy way:

A **giant pink kite** with a smiley face dropped from the sky.

Without hesitation, I grabbed its string.

And within seconds – I was soaring.

Free from mirrors.

Free from swords.

Free from giant hammers and throbbing toes.

Just air.

Altitude.

And me.

And just when I was beginning to enjoy the ride. . .

Whoosh.

I landed – gently – in a **miniature greenhouse**.

Soft light. Warm air. Tiny plants sprouting.

Something about it made me feel held, grounded, and oddly safe.

I sat.

I breathed.

And for the first time that day. . .

I got it.

🧭 FUTURE YOU RETURNS – "Let Me Explain. . ."

Future You pauses after telling the story.

You're looking at them, half-stunned, half-smiling.

Then they say:

"What just happened, that surreal trip through my subconscious, was a metaphor."

"A message."

"A mind-map."

"My life showed me the path to sustainable growth – through five powerful truths:"

🔄 THE FIVE OBJECTS REAPPEAR

Now they're glowing.

1. **S – Self-Reflection** → (🔘 **A Mirror**)
2. **M – Mastery** → (⚔ **A Samurai Sword**)
3. **I – Implementation** → (🔨 **A Hammer**)
4. **L – Liberation** → (🪁 **A Kite**)
5. **E – Environment** → (🏡 **A Greenhouse**)

You blink, confused.

Future You picks them up, one by one.

💡 THE SMILE FRAMEWORK

✳ S – Self-Reflection → *The Mirror*

I cannot grow what I won't face.

The mirror forced me to *look* – really look – at who I was, how I thought, what I believed, and what I'd been avoiding.

This is where transformation begins:

In radical, often uncomfortable honesty.

🥷 M – Mastery → *The Samurai Sword*

Mastery is my edge. My discipline.

The Samurai sword represented the sharpness of my focus, the consistency of my routines, and the honour in self-discipline.

I didn't stumble into greatness.

I carved it – one swing at a time.

↖ I – Implementation → *The Hammer*

Ideas without action are just decoration.

The hammer was my tool of execution.

It built, it broke, it reinforced.

This is where "someday" became "now."

I may have stubbed my toe in the process – but progress is always messy.

No swings, no results.

⚘ L – Liberation → *The Kite*

I couldn't heal in the same place that hurt me.

Sometimes, I needed to rise above.

Let go.

The kite was about emotional release – freeing myself from perfectionism, control, guilt, and shame.

Real liberation didn't just feel light – it *was* light.

❧ E – Environment → *The Greenhouse*

Nothing grows without the right conditions.

The greenhouse represented my space, my circle, and my systems.

I wasn't weak for struggling in toxic environments – I was just *misplaced*.

Growth requires nurture, not noise.

✸ FUTURE YOU – THE FINAL MESSAGE

"So now you see it."

"The mirror. The sword. The hammer. The kite. The greenhouse."

"It wasn't just a dream."

"It's your *design*."

"The warehouse showed you what's been *costing* your joy."

"The SMILE Framework shows you how to *redeem* it."

A Note from Jackson

Let's look at the SMILE Framework in a little more detail and why each of these objects is so essential to programming your new default app.

S – Self-Reflection → *The Mirror*

The mirror represents that long hard look at yourself. This is an *essential* first step. Before you do anything else. Because before you can change anything, you need to look and see where you're going wrong.

This can be confronting. You might be afraid of what you'll see. But persevere. Look at your reflection. Take stock.

Many people try to "fix" the problems in their lives but skip this step. The result? They go in the wrong direction. Waste valuable time and energy chasing solutions that aren't what they need. Feel disheartened and slip into old patterns.

Hold the mirror up to yourself.

Truly look at what it's showing you.

Then move forward from a place of recognition.

M – Mastery → *The Samurai Sword*

The Samurai sword represents the decision to start working on yourself. To pursue mastery. We all know that a Samurai underwent years of gruelling training. Not just physical. Mental. Emotional. They committed to a lifetime of growth and constant learning.

Committing to live your life based on growth is not an overnight fix. It's a slow process. The sword represents the training process for the art of being present.

Pick it up.

Commit to growth.

I – Implementation → *The Hammer*

Every now and then, a sword is too delicate a tool for the job at hand. This is when you need the hammer. It's there for when you have to make drastic decisions. Break through.

Once you've developed strength from consistent training with your sword, you might need to turn to a heavier implement to hammer some things out. This is the doing.

Mastery can feel overwhelming, but with a hammer you can do what's needed. Break old patterns. It's all about going from AWARENESS to ACTION.

Be prepared to use it when you hit a wall.

L – Liberation → *The Kite*

The kite symbolises the decision to take a wider view of your life. The 50,000 ft. view of the world. To give you access to a place of freedom.

Just as the houses and cars look tiny when you take off in an aeroplane and climb higher, so too do your problems and challenges look smaller and more manageable when you view them from a broader perspective.

The kite allows you to take a different view of your life.

Gain a new perspective.

And see alternative paths.

E – Environment → *The Greenhouse*

The greenhouse represents not only an environment in which you can thrive, but also a space that protects what you've grown. What you've discovered.

Your peace.

Your heart.

Only with this protected, safe space can you ensure you avoid the same traumatic cycles you were trapped in before.

Plant the seeds.

Tend the seedlings.

Watch your heart blossom.

Jackson's Journey Through SMILE

I have been through this process myself.

The Day I Pulled Over (and Everything Changed)

A SMILE journey

I didn't step away because I was burnt out.

I stepped away because I was becoming numb.

For weeks, maybe months, there had been signs I didn't want to acknowledge.

Persistent headaches that never fully went away.

A low, floating pressure behind my eyes, like a cloud that followed me everywhere.

Frustration without a clear cause.

Overwhelm that lingered even after rest.

And then there were the habits.

Workouts quietly disappeared.

Patience shortened.

Joy flattened.

Sugar became a coping mechanism rather than a choice.

Endless scrolling filled the gaps where silence should have lived.

On the outside, everything still looked fine.

The diary was full.

Business was moving.

Opportunities were there.

But internally, something was drifting slowly, subtly, dangerously.

S – Self-Reflection

The first moment that truly disturbed me came when I realised I didn't want to go to a keynote.

That was new.

I love keynotes.

I love teaching.

I love being on stage inside organisations, on platforms, with people.

Energy, ideas, connection – that's my natural environment.

But this time, I felt nothing.

No excitement.

No nerves.

No anticipation.

Just a quiet despondence.

A strange disconnect.

That was the moment self-reflection kicked in not as an exercise, but as an alarm.

I realised I was close to an edge. I hadn't fallen off but was near enough to feel the drop.

Like a storm forming just out of sight.

I couldn't yet name it, but my body already had.

Then came the morning that changed everything.

I had just dropped my daughters off at school.

The usual noise of the school run faded mums and dads, engines starting, gates closing.

One by one, the cars pulled away.

I stayed.

Sitting there alone in the car park, something heavy settled in my chest.

Not panic.

Not anxiety.

Grief.

A deep, quiet grief.

It felt like a separation. Like I had stepped away from something familiar but hadn't yet arrived anywhere new.

There was an awkwardness to it.

A discomfort.

Almost like mourning, except I couldn't yet explain what I was mourning.

In that stillness, self-reflection became unavoidable.

The headaches.

The pressure.

The constant output.

The noise.

And then a single, clarifying thought cut through everything:

If I don't stop now, something inside me is going to break.

M – Mastery

What followed wasn't instant peace; it was heaviness.

I stepped away from everything for 61 days.

Business.

Social media.

Content.

Constant movement.

At first, the silence felt wrong.

Unproductive.

Awkward.

Silence has weight when you're not used to it.

It exposes what busyness hides.

And what it exposed in me was how much of my identity had been tied to output rather than alignment.

This was the beginning of mastery. Not mastering productivity, but mastering awareness.

I began to observe myself instead of judging myself.

To notice patterns instead of fighting them.

To sit with discomfort instead of numbing it.

The grief from that car-park moment lingered.

So did the awkwardness of shedding an old version of myself.

But something subtle began to shift.

As the days passed, the headaches softened.

The mental fog lifted.

Clarity returned.

Mastery, I realised, wasn't about control.

It was about understanding.

I – Implementation

With awareness came action but not the kind I was used to.

Instead of rushing back into output, I implemented different rhythms.

Prayer.

Fasting.

Meditation.

Stillness.

Not as religious routines, but as grounding practices.

Implementation at this stage wasn't about doing more; it was about doing *what aligned.*

Returning deliberately to what I believe is true, not just what is urgent.

Day by day, I felt myself becoming more present.

More centred.

More intentional.

The difference was noticeable not just emotionally, but physically.

The constant background pressure eased.

My thinking sharpened.

My attention lengthened.

L – Liberation

Liberation came quietly.

Not as a breakthrough moment, but as a decision.

A decision to let go of old motivations.

To stop feeding the need for constant validation.

To die – daily – to ego-driven urgency.

Liberation meant allowing the pruning without resisting it.

Trusting that what was falling away needed to fall away.

It was humbling.

But it was freeing.

I realised I wasn't losing momentum; I was shedding weight.

E – (Environment)

By the time I returned, I knew one thing clearly:

This new version of me needed protecting.

Alignment is fragile if the environment isn't right.

So I began shaping a greenhouse around my life.

New boundaries.

Slower rhythms.

Intentional silence.

Healthier inputs.

Not to retreat from the world, but to remain whole *within* it.

Looking back now, I see it clearly:

That moment in the car park wasn't weakness.

It was self-reflection.

The silence wasn't avoidance.

It was mastery.

The practices weren't escape.

They were implementation.

The surrender wasn't loss.

It was liberation.

And the life I'm now designing is the greenhouse that sustains it all.

Stepping away didn't cost me who I was.

It helped me remember.

I realised I was chasing dreams that weren't mine.

For me, mastery also involved understanding neuroscience, because the better I understand how my brain works on a chemical level, the easier I find it to handle my emotions. Now I can step back and see: this is my amygdala. I need a bit of oxytocin.

And I know how to correct those imbalances.

If my oxytocin is depleted, that's a sign to give my wife a hug.

We all need multiple masters who we can tap into. A financial master. An adventure master. A relationship master. A spiritual master. A chaos master even.

But mastery is only valuable if we also implement. You can reflect all you want, but if you never act on your reflections, nothing will change.

For me, implementation was a commitment to that 61-day process to strip everything back. It was a hammer blow to my life. Dramatic. Shattering habits. Pre-conceptions.

But in the process of breaking down, I discovered space. Silence. Stillness.

And from this stillness came liberation.

I let go of the person *the world told me I needed to be* and instead started to work on *becoming the best version of myself.* I soared above with the kite. I looked down on my life. And I could see, with clarity, what I needed to do.

The Gift of Freedom

For me, freedom is a birthright of all human beings. It's the anchor that holds you when you face life's challenges. But freedom is also a gift. And that's what I'm protecting.

To do that, I need to make some changes to my environment. I'm going to hire a social media manager for my business so I don't get sucked into apps for hours on end. Scrolling. Losing who I am in the feed.

This also stems from what I've learnt about neuroscience. Our brains have what are known as mirror neurons, and we reflect the people we are closest to.

Science supports this.

When you put yourself in the right environment, you will be motivated.

Your environment isn't just physical. It's mental. It's spiritual. Tend to all of them.

Change your physical environment by going for a walk.

Change your mental environment by consuming content that allows you to mentally escape where you are if you can't physically change your environment in that moment.

Change your spiritual environment by meditating or praying.

I now do all of these things regularly. Because I know that when I'm in the right environment, life flows. Adventure happens. Joy is visible all around.

Ultimately, the SMILE Framework helps you become your own saviour.

When you save yourself, you start to save the world. One person at a time.

⊘ Mirror Time: Pre-SMILE Reflection

> ### ? Journal Prompt
> *Out of the 14 doors. . .*
> *Which three felt most familiar?*
> *Why?*
> This is the pause. It's not the end, not yet.

It's the inhale before the action.

You might be feeling seen. Or you might be feeling attacked. Both are valid.

But I want you to know something powerful:

By making it here. . .

You've already started your transformation.

Now let's get back to the action. . .

Act III, Scene 2
Living with a Smile

I was cleaning recently – not because I suddenly love cleaning.

Because it resets me.

There's something about clearing physical space that clears mental space. It's rhythmic. Intentional. Quietly satisfying. A small dopamine release without chaos attached to it.

And while I'm cleaning, I'm listening to an audiobook:

Your Mind Believes What You Think.

Powerful title.

Uncomfortable title.

Because it implies something dangerous:

If my life feels limited . . . my thinking might be responsible.

There's a section in the book that stops me mid-wipe.

It talks about **homeostasis**.

Let's break that down.

Homeostasis is your body's natural tendency to stay the same.

Temperature.

Heart rate.

Chemistry.

Identity.

Your system is designed to preserve familiarity.

Not progress.

And that's where most people get blindsided.

Because when you try to become someone new – more disciplined, more peaceful, more confident, more focused – your nervous system interprets it as a threat.

"Who are you becoming?"

"This isn't familiar."

"This isn't safe."

Your brain doesn't care about your goals.

It cares about predictability.

So, when you attempt a new identity overnight – wake up at 4 a.m., cut out sugar, delete social media, rewrite your entire personality – your system panics.

Not because you can't change.

But because you're trying to leap beyond your biological comfort zone.

And homeostasis pulls you back.

Gently.

Subtly.

Relentlessly.

That's why most transformations fail in week two.

Not from lack of desire.

From biological resistance.

So what's the solution?

Subtlety.

Momentary shifts.

Small, repeated interruptions.

Not revolution.

Recalibration.

And this is where journaling becomes powerful.

Not as emotional venting.

As neurological training.

Because when I journal, I'm doing three things at once:

1. I'm documenting pattern.
2. I'm slowing reaction into reflection.
3. I'm programming identity through language.

Your brain is not your enemy.

It's an imaging machine.

It runs the pictures you feed it.

If I repeatedly write:

"I always mess this up."

"I'm not disciplined."

"That's just who I am."

My mind believes it.

Because your mind believes what you think.

But if I begin writing:

"I notice the urge."

"I pause before reacting."

"I choose differently today."

Now I am subtly introducing a new identity.

And because it's subtle – not dramatic – my nervous system doesn't rebel.

It adapts.

That's the genius of the 66-day journal.

It doesn't try to overthrow the old self in one night.

It interrupts it quietly.

Again.

And again.

And again.

Until the new behaviour feels normal.

Until homeostasis resets at a higher level.

Because here's the truth:

You are already becoming something every day.

The only question is whether you're becoming it consciously.

Journaling forces awareness.

And awareness is leverage.

It allows you to become an expert in pattern recognition.

You catch yourself mid-scroll.

Mid-complaint.

Mid-"yes."

Mid-guilt.

Mid-comparison.

That microsecond of awareness?

That's where identity shifts.

Your brain isn't against you.

It's loyal to what you repeat.

Program it wisely.

The version of you on this journey keeps a journal not a soft diary, but a record of resistance against the 14 bad habits eroding your joy.

Each entry carries defiance.

Each page reflects resilience.

It reads like territory reclaimed.

Like a series of small battles fought and won not out in the world, but in the mind.

The 66-Day Redemption Journal

Living with a Smile

(Extracts from My Journal)

Day 1 – 6:10 a.m. – Bedroom

I wake up.

The warehouse is still in my bones.

The doors.

The mirrors.

The uncomfortable honesty.

I lie there for a second and notice something.

My default is still there.

The reflexes haven't disappeared overnight.

But I have.

I sit upright.

I decide.

For the next 66 days, I am not drifting.

No more accidental living.

No more rehearsed reactions.

No more blaming "circumstances."

This is my journal.

This is what it looks like when I stop sleepwalking.

---

1. Say YES to Everything

Day 10 – 7:42 a.m. – Kitchen

My phone lights up.

"Can you help with this tomorrow?"

My nervous system answers before my brain does.

Yes.

Yes.

Say yes. Be helpful. Be needed. Be liked.

I watch the script trying to run.

It's almost funny.

I pause.

Language matters.

Instead of "Of course!! ☺"

I type:

"I can't commit to that tomorrow."

I stare at it.

It feels rebellious.

I press send.

My chest tightens. Cortisol flares for a second.

Then something else arrives.

Space.

I realise I've been addicted to being needed.

Today I choose being aligned.

---

2. Crave Other People's Attention
Day 14 – 6:18 a.m. – Bedside

The alarm goes off.

My thumb reaches for the phone like it has a mind of its own.

The scroll.

The numbers.

The tiny red notifications whispering, "You exist."

I stop mid-reach.

It's mechanical.

Almost embarrassing.

I sit up instead.

No scrolling.

No audience.

No applause.

Silence feels awkward at first.

Then clean.

If my mood depends on other people reacting to me before I've even brushed my teeth, that's not freedom.

Today I reclaim the first five minutes of my life.

---

3. Cancel Special Occasions with Family

Day 20 – 4:35 p.m. – Park Bench

I leave work on time.

My brain tries one last trick.

"You could just send that email . . ."

No.

I am sitting in a park now.

Ice cream dripping onto my fingers.

Someone laughs beside me.

And I realise how often I've traded moments for "just one more task."

Satire hits me.

Imagine explaining on my deathbed:

"I missed your childhood because . . . inbox."

Today I am not half-present.

Today I am here.

Fully.

---

4. Don't Workout at All

Day 23 – 6:03 a.m. – Living Room Floor

I do not feel like moving.

Let's not romanticise it.

My body wants the duvet.

My mind suggests negotiation.

"Start tomorrow."

"You've earned a break."

"You're busy."

I smile.

I've heard this voice before.

I drop to the floor.

Twelve minutes.

No cinematic soundtrack.

Just breath. Effort. Resistance.

My body warms up.

My mind sharpens.

Discipline doesn't shout.

It accumulates.

---

5. Create Time for Toxic People
Day 27 – 8:12 p.m. – Sofa

A name flashes.

My body reacts instantly.

That slight contraction in my chest.

I notice it.

Awareness used to arrive after the damage.

Now it arrives before.

I don't reply immediately.

I don't justify.

I don't explain my boundaries like a court case.

I let the phone sit.

Access to me is no longer automatic.

Peace is not negotiable.

---

6. Overthink Everything

Day 31 – 1:15 p.m. – Outside Café

I type a message.

I delete it.

I retype it.

I add a comma.

I remove the comma.

I laugh.

This is absurd.

"Would be great to catch up."

Send.

My stomach flips.

But I don't spiral.

Perfectionism disguises itself as intelligence.

Today I choose courage over clever wording.

---

7. Chase Perfection Relentlessly

Day 36 – 9:40 p.m. – Friend's Kitchen

Sauce lands on my white shirt.

Of course it does.

Old me would panic. Apologise. Withdraw.

Instead, I laugh.

I let the stain exist.

Messy is honest.

The need to look flawless is exhausting.

Tonight I let humanity breathe.

---

8. Make a Grudge List

Day 40 – 7:55 p.m. – Living Room

An old memory surfaces.

I feel the familiar invitation to rehearse it.

To replay the injustice.

To polish it.

I stop.

Grudges are heavy luggage.

And I've been dragging them into rooms that have nothing to do with the original story.

I release it.

Not because they deserve it.

Because I deserve peace.

---

9. Be Guided by Guilt

Day 44 – 10:02 p.m. – Desk

I almost say yes out of obligation.

I almost stay small out of guilt.

Guilt sounds noble.

But it's fear in a tuxedo.

I choose alignment instead.

I click confirm.

Growth requires leaving rooms I've outgrown.

---

10. Buy Personal Development Books and Don't Read Them

Day 48 – 7:12 a.m. – Study

The bookshelf stares back at me.

Spines untouched.

Titles screaming "Become Better."

I open one.

I read one chapter.

I implement one idea.

No dopamine from accumulation.

Only transformation from action.

Information without implementation is intellectual junk food.

Today I eat real food.

---

11. Compare Yourself to Everyone

Day 52 – 7:36 p.m. – Kitchen

I scroll.

Someone else is winning.

The comparison thought knocks.

"You're behind."

I close the app.

Comparison is a thief disguised as motivation.

Their timeline is not my timetable.

I return to my life.

Mine feels sufficient.

---

12. Complain About Everything
Day 56 – 9:05 a.m. – Office Desk

"How was your weekend?"

I almost default to sarcasm.

To cynicism.

To the easy complaint.

Instead, I say what's good.

Because there is good.

Complaining used to bond me to mediocrity.

Gratitude bonds me to growth.

Later, I take action instead of narrating dissatisfaction again.

---

13. Avoid Delegation at All Costs
Day 60 – 6:18 p.m. – Home Office

"I've got it" sits on my tongue.

I swallow it.

"Can you help with that?"

The sky does not fall.

The house does not crumble.

Strength is not doing everything.

Strength is knowing what only I should do.

Everything else can move.

---

14. Glorify Busyness
Day 63 – 8:49 p.m. – Living Room, Lights Low

I check tomorrow's calendar.

Two meetings.

Space.

Old me would panic-fill it.

Send emails. Schedule calls. Manufacture urgency.

I close the laptop.

I sit.

No productivity theatre.

No hustle badge.

No dramatic exhaustion story.

Stillness feels mature.

Busyness used to be my identity.

Now it is optional.

When I look in the mirror now, I see someone sharper.

Not louder.

Sharper.

More aware of language.

More aware of reflex.

More aware of patterns.

I see:

The version who says no without flinching.

The version who shows up fully.

The version who moves when it's inconvenient.

The version who rests without guilt.

The version who releases instead of rehearses.

The doors are still there.

But they are no longer entrances.

They are reminders.

The warehouse begins to dissolve.

This time, I am not afraid.

Because I am no longer living by default.

I am living by design.

And as I approach the day of my final verdict, (Day 66) I feel something unexpected.

Confidence.

Not arrogance.

Evidence.

Sixty-six days of intentional disruption.

Sixty-six days of choosing differently.

I know what the outcome will be.

Because I am no longer the same person who walked into that warehouse.

[FADE TO BLACK]

Jornal entry: **The Morning of the Final Verdict**

It's still dark when I wake up.

No alarm.

No jolt.

Just awareness.

There's something different in the air. I can feel it before I can explain it. A quiet electricity beneath the surface. Not anxiety. Not anticipation. Something steadier.

Clarity.

I don't reach for my phone.

That would have been the old reflex.

Instead, I sit up slowly in bed and set a timer.

Seven minutes.

Seven minutes of silence.

Not scrolling.

Not planning.

Not rehearsing.

Just silence.

The first few seconds feel noisy. My brain, loyal as ever, attempts to flood me with thoughts. To-do lists. What-ifs. Fragments of old narratives trying to regain ground.

I notice them.

I don't wrestle them.

I let them pass.

This is recalibration.

Seven minutes is longer than it sounds when you're fully present. My nervous system settles. My breathing deepens. I begin to focus deliberately on gratitude – not vague gratitude, but specific gratitude.

The last 66 days.

The no's I said.

The workouts I completed.

The grudges I released.

The comparisons I interrupted.

The boundaries I held.

The stillness I embraced.

I feel it.

Not pride.

Evidence.

The resistance is still there. It hasn't disappeared. It still whispers occasionally. Still tries to negotiate. Still offers comfort in old patterns.

But I am no longer owned by it.

That's the difference.

I understand now that growth doesn't eliminate resistance – it outgrows it.

I open my eyes before the timer ends.

The room is the same.

But I am not.

There was a time when my mornings were dictated by urgency. Emails. Notifications. Invisible pressure from a world addicted to motion without awareness.

Now I see it for what it is.

The lie.

The lie that busyness equals value.

The lie that reaction equals relevance.

The lie that exhaustion equals importance.

The lie that it's normal to drift.

I understand something deeper now – zombification.

The process of moving through life unconscious. Reacting. Responding. Consuming. Without reflection.

Walking, but asleep.

Scrolling, but unaware.

Speaking, but not intentional.

I was never broken.

I was automated.

And over the last 66 days, I have been waking up.

The timer ends.

Soft chime.

I stretch slowly, deliberately. I move with awareness. There is no rush. I step onto the living room floor.

Twelve minutes.

That's all.

The body protests lightly. It always does in the first 30 seconds.

"Skip it."

"You deserve rest."

"You'll be fine without it."

I smile.

This voice is familiar.

I begin anyway.

Push-ups. Squats. Breath steady. Focus sharp.

It's not about aesthetics anymore. It's about agency.

Every rep is a message to my nervous system:

I am in control.

By minute eight, my body is warm. By minute 12, I feel aligned. Not hyped. Not over-stimulated.

Aligned.

I pause.

Inhale.

Exhale.

There's a steadiness in me that didn't exist before the 66 days. Not because today is special.

But because the repetition has built something durable.

I walk into the shower.

Warm water first.

Steam fills the space.

The shower used to be autopilot – think about the day, rush through the motions, replay imaginary conversations.

Now I pay attention.

To the temperature.

To the sound of water against tile.

To my breathing.

And then, as I've done for weeks now, I turn the dial.

Cold.

Sixty seconds.

The first rush hits like a shockwave. My breath wants to spike. My body wants to retreat.

But I stay.

I've learned something about cold exposure.

It's not just physical discipline.

It's nervous system training.

Cold teaches you to remain calm under discomfort.

To regulate instead of react.

Thirty seconds in.

The shock fades.

There's clarity in the cold.

Forty-five seconds.

I breathe deeper.

Sixty.

I turn the dial back.

And I laugh quietly to myself.

There was a version of me who would have called this extreme. Unnecessary. Performative.

Now it's practice.

Micro-evidence that I can stay present when discomfort arrives.

I dry off slowly.

There is no frantic energy.

No invisible pressure.

No underlying panic.

This day was always going to be good.

Not because of what is about to happen.

Because of what has already happened.

Sixty-six days of choosing differently.

Sixty-six days of pattern interruption.

Sixty-six days of language correction.

Sixty-six days of noticing.

That's what changes a person.

Not hype.

Repetition.

I look in the mirror.

I don't see perfection.

I see sharpness.

Awareness.

Intentionality.

I see someone who no longer confuses noise with progress.

Someone who understands that the mind is not an enemy – it is an imaging machine.

Feed it chaos, it creates chaos.

Feed it clarity, it creates structure.

And over these last weeks, I have been feeding it clarity.

I button my shirt.

There's no dramatic soundtrack in the background.

No swelling orchestral score.

Just quiet certainty.

The final verdict doesn't intimidate me.

Because the real verdict has already been delivered.

In the morning I chose silence over scrolling.

In the workout I chose discipline over delay.

In the cold I chose regulation over reaction.

This is not about a courtroom anymore.

This is about identity.

I am not being pulled to and fro by every headline, every opinion, every emotional fluctuation.

I am aware.

And awareness is power.

I understand now that society runs on distraction. On urgency. On comparison. On endless consumption.

But I have tasted something different.

Presence.

And once you taste presence, you don't crave chaos the same way.

I step towards the door.

There's no fear.

There's anticipation – but it's clean.

I know this version of me.

Stronger.

Sharper.

Not because life got easier.

Because I got intentional.

Sixty-six days ago, I walked into a warehouse uncertain.

Today, I walk forward certain.

Not unstoppable because I am loud.

Unstoppable because I am regulated.

Ready to claim back my life.

Ready for the verdict.

And whatever comes next.

Act III, Scene 3

The SMILE Framework –
an Interlude with Jackson

The SMILE Framework isn't something you have to apply all in one go.

In fact, I strongly advise you *not* to do that.

Taking on too much, too quickly only leads to overwhelm. Which is the opposite of what we're trying to achieve.

The key is taking it slowly. Implementing step by step.

Pausing to notice how it makes you feel. And how it impacts those around you.

In Act IV, I'll share the full 66 Day Redemption Challenge with you. But for now, here are some small, simple steps you can take within each element of the SMILE Framework to help you get started.

Remember the journey isn't just for 66 days though.

It's for the rest of your life.

There will be days when you want to quit.

Days where it feels like it's not working.

Days where nothing seems to make sense.

Trust the process.

Self-Reflection

This is the foundation for everything that will follow. You can't change your situation without honestly acknowledging where you are. Confront the truth of your life. Embrace it.

Then move forward.

The simplest way I've found to begin your journey is with gratitude.

No matter how hopeless or hard life feels, my challenge to you is to find one thing, right now, that you're grateful for.

Here's an easy one: that you're reading this book. Either you care enough about yourself to have bought it, or someone else cares enough about you to have bought it for you.

Go a step further. Be grateful for the education you received that taught you to read.

Journaling is really helpful throughout this process. Even if all you do is write down what you did each day.

You can use the self-reflection questions from each of the chapters in Act II as prompts.

Mastery

Mastery is simply about introducing something new to your life.

I chose roller skating because it's a nice metaphor for the whole process.

When you start, even the ground beneath your feet feels unstable.

It's hard.

It's uncomfortable.

It's scary.

But then. . . It's wonderful.

All of a sudden, the fear dissolves.

You're truly present.

You're enjoying being in the moment.

Gliding around the rink.

I know because I did this. I learnt to roller skate and I kid you not, the first couple of sessions I could think of nothing else but keeping stable. It grounded me in the present moment. But when you learn to skate properly, it's beautiful.

Choose something that is challenging but that you want to do.

It could be a course in public speaking.

Or a course to help you better manage your finances.

Or a relationship course.

What it is doesn't matter.

The purpose is to choose a new skill or hobby and dedicate time and energy to mastering it.

Implementation

Here's the thing, you will only reach the beautiful part of that process if you show up.

Take action.

Keep going.

Don't stop, even when you feel resistance.

Don't let the doubts in your mind override the desire to learn something new and step outside of your comfort zone.

I have paid a friend £500 to help hold me accountable. The deal was, if I didn't do what I said I would five times, they got to keep the money.

If you know you'll struggle to take action by yourself, find a way to push yourself to do it.

Get a friend to go with you to the course.

Pay a friend to hold you accountable like I did.

Share your plans more broadly with a group of friends, knowing that they'll ask you about them.

Do whatever you need to make sure you take action and continue taking action.

Liberation

Liberation is less about physical freedom and more about an internal resolve that you will never again be affected by someone else's BS.

The best way I've found to do this is to come up with my own liberation statement, like a manifesto or personal creed that sets out **the kind of person I'm becoming**.

For example: "I will not be sucked in by negativity. I will not be affected by the small, negative voice in my head."

When you read your liberation statement back to yourself, it is liberating because it reminds you of who you are choosing to become.

You become, then you behave.

It's essential to take an active role in choosing who you want to become, because the script you follow determines the character you become.

Part of my personal creed is that I never say, "I'm tired."

Instead, I'll say, "I need an energy top-up." Because I believe in the power of words.

When you start to flip your own script, you will become hyper aware of how others around you are following more negative scripts. In some cases, you might want to let those negative people leave your life. But don't rush to judgement.

Remember that it has taken you time – 66 days – to get to this place. Perhaps the other person who is complaining hasn't started their journey yet. Approaching those people with a bit of grace and empathy could help them follow their own redemption journey. Your role is to hold space and bring correction when necessary. Slowly and lovingly. But **connect before you correct.**

Connection will allow you to introduce correction gently. In a way that the other person is receptive to.

Understand that often complaints or negativity come from a place of fear. Create safe spaces. Watch what unfolds when you do.

Another part of my personal creed is, "I will not judge negative people because I was once like them."

The second you decide not to judge at all, your internal resistance to the process starts to dissolve. And the moment you decide not to judge the outer world, your inner world becomes stronger.

You're creating an inner fortress. This process is less about what other people say to you and more about what you say to yourself, which in turn determines what you become.

What might surprise you is that as you enter your becoming, the people around you will either try to match your frequency or they'll fall away.

Environment

This is about your physical and mental environment. And here's what's great: Your greenhouse can be whatever you want it to be.

I'm serious.

There are so many ways to create greenhouse moments in your day.

They don't require time.

Or money.

All you need to do is decide what your greenhouse will be.

Here are some of my greenhouse moments:

- Sitting in my car for 20 minutes after I drop my girls at school.
- Time in the shower.

- A flight, where I can't use my phone.
- Five minutes in any space without technology.

Take a moment to think about where you could introduce greenhouse moments in your day.

If you commute, can your train ride become a greenhouse moment? Instead of getting frustrated by the crowds, take a book. Absorb yourself in reading. Greenhouse moment.

Find a weird space in your home – a closet, under the bed – and take yourself there for 30 seconds. No phone. No distractions. Greenhouse moment.

Singing along to your favourite song (loudly) when you're alone in your car. Greenhouse moment.

Wearing your favourite jumper might make you feel good or comforted. Greenhouse moment.

I have a pair of trainers that, when I wear them, I feel different. It might not be shoes for you. It might be jewellery. A scarf. A specific shirt. Lean into that greenhouse moment.

Too many of us are overloaded and overwhelmed in life. It's probably why you're reading this book. So **Keep It Simple!**

What about a favourite mug – drinking from it can become a greenhouse moment. (This idea came from my editor Kat, who told me she once cried when she broke her favourite mug. It took her three months to find another one. Why? Because we can find a visceral kind of comfort in these everyday objects.)

Think about it from another perspective. . .

When you were a child, what was your favourite toy? I bet it was a bit battered. Probably dirty. Certainly less than perfect. And you took it everywhere with you. But what would have happened if someone had bought a new, identical version of that toy? Would it have been the same? No.

The *emotional association* with the item is what we love. Not the item itself.

For too many adults, the toys of our childhood have been replaced by our phones.

Put your phone to one side and ask yourself now, what's your "toy" as an adult?

What brings you emotional comfort when you use it or wear it?

How can you lean into that to help introduce some simple greenhouse moments to your days?

SMILE

If you really don't know where to start, start with a smile.

I'm serious.

It's amazing how different you feel if you smile, even when you don't want to.

And you'll see the energy in those around you shifting too.

Now, remember the 14 doors we visited? It's time to take a peek at what life is like after implementing the SMILE Framework. Let's jump back in. . .

 Act III, Scene 4
The Return to the
Warehouse

DAY 66 – 7 a.m.

[INT. THE CENTRE OF THE WAREHOUSE – THE 14 DOORS ARE GLOWING]

You're back in the warehouse.

Only this time it feels less oppressive.

Lighter somehow.

Future You is waiting patiently.

FUTURE YOU (smiling):

"Are you ready to revisit your 14 friends?"

"We won't stay as long with them this time. . ."

211

"But seeing how they're getting on might help you understand how far you've come."

You take a deep breath.

You're not sure you're ready for this, but you nod.

Future You guides you towards the first door. . .

🏠 Door 1 Opens: Layla – The Overcommitter

Layla stands in her kitchen. Phone in hand.

The house looks tidier than you remember.

She's speaking into her phone.

> *"Sorry sis. I can't commit to that tomorrow, I've already got a full day. Maybe next week if you can give me a bit more notice."*

She hits send. Then smiles.

[FADE TO BLACK]

🏠 Door 2 Opens: Jordan – The Performer

You open the door to Jordan being embraced by his partner.

He's crying.

But he looks relaxed.

"You're not mad?" he's asking.

"Of course not, you tried, that's all I ever ask. We all make mistakes."

Jordan nods.

Hugs his partner again, this time with a smile.

[FADE TO BLACK]

🏠 Door 3 Opens: Mel – The No-Show

Mel isn't at home.

They're in the park with a child.

Eating huge ice creams.

Sticky fingers and faces.

"Can we go on the see-saw?"

Mel grins.

"Of course, I'll race you there!"

They sprint away from you, laughing.

[FADE TO BLACK]

🏠 Door 4 Opens: Chris – The Tired Achiever

Chris is exiting his apartment as you get there.

He's lost weight.

His skin looks brighter.

His gym bag is slung over one shoulder.

There's a protein shake in his other hand.

You watch him bounce down the stairs, looking ten years younger.

[FADE TO BLACK]

🏠 Door 5 Opens: Kelly – The Peacekeeper

"I'm not coming to the pub on Sunday," Kelly is saying.

"Babe, why not?" her boyfriend asks.

"Because I've booked a spa day," she replies with a smile.

"I thought you liked going to the pub?"

"Sometimes. But not every Sunday," her tone firm but warm.

[FADE TO BLACK]

🏠 Door 6 Opens: Isaac – The Analyst

Isaac is typing a message on his phone.

Concentrating. Focused.

He pauses. Deletes a sentence. Retypes it.

> *"Hey, sorry I've been MIA. Would be great to meet up soon."*

Hits send.

He looks panicked. Then his phone pings.

> *"Would love to catch up. You free Saturday?"*

Isaac smiles.

"Sure, 3pm?" Hits send. No second thoughts

[FADE TO BLACK]

⊞ Door 7 Opens: Camille – The Flawless One

Camille is eating pizza with a friend.

Laughing. Happy.

As she grabs a slice, tomato sauce drips from the end of the pizza straight onto her white blouse.

She reaches for a napkin, dabs it, then gives up.

Instead, she grabs her phone and takes a selfie with her friend. Stained blouse in full view.

Types the caption, *"Fun with my bestie."* Hits "Share."

No second thoughts. No need for perfect. Messy is more than good enough.

[FADE TO BLACK]

⊞ Door 8 Opens: Ray – The Collector

Ray isn't in his basement.

He's outside a registry office. Wearing a suit.

Laughing and chatting to other wedding guests.

He grabs a handful of confetti as the basket is passed around.

Throws it in the air over the happy couple walking down the steps.

He joins the reception line. The groom leans in to give him a warm hug.

"So pleased you could make it mate, means the world."

Ray hugs him back.

"Wouldn't have missed it."

[FADE TO BLACK]

🏛 Door 9 Opens: Elias – The Weight Bearer

Elias stands in his apartment, passport in one hand. Suitcases by the door.

He taps his phone. Opens an app.

Plenty of time to make his flight to New York.

You spot a card on his sideboard. Lean over to read it.

> *"Congratulations on the promotion! Can't believe you're moving to New York!"*

Elias takes a deep breath.

No more standing still. He's moving up.

[FADE TO BLACK]

🏛 Door 10 Opens: Tara – The Librarian

Tara is on a Zoom call.

She's furiously scribbling notes.

A book lies open next to her, with sticky notes poking out of the pages.

"Tara, I just wanted to congratulate you on your essay from last week. Excellent work. I can see you really absorbed the content from the module. . ." the voice from the screen is saying.

Tara beams.

"I feel like I've learnt so much already, and we're only two months in," she replies with a smile.

[FADE TO BLACK]

🏠 Door 11 Opens: James – The Approval Addict

James walks into his apartment and tosses his keys on the table.

He sets his phone down next to them, then starts making dinner.

But he seems to stand taller than last time you saw him.

As you watch, his phone stays silent.

He doesn't scroll.

There's a knock on the door.

He opens it to a friend holding a pack of beers.

"Perfect mate, dinner's on the go. . ."

They each crack open a beer and start chatting.

No phones.

No social media.

No quick snaps for the ';gram.

Just presence.

[FADE TO BLACK]

🏠 Door 12 Opens: Gavin – The Professional Whiner

Gavin's already at his desk, working away.

A colleague walks past. Pauses to offer him a coffee.

"How was your weekend, Gavin?"

He looks up. Mug in hand.

"You know what, it was great, thanks. Got out with my sister and her kids for the day to make the most of the sunshine. How about you?"

His colleague smiles.

"You know, it was pretty low key, but it was nice to have some sun. Usual coffee?"

Gavin nods.

Returns to his email.

Re-reads his resignation letter, then hits "Send."

[FADE TO BLACK]

🏠 Door 13 Opens: Melissa – The Martyr Manager

Melissa is at her laptop in her home office.

She's typing an email while checking the time out of the corner of her eye.

Her partner pops their head round her door.

"Need a hand with anything?"

"Actually, could you go and pick up the kids from their dance class? That'll give me time to finish these emails. . ."

"Sure. I'll pick up dinner on the way home so you don't have to cook."

Melissa is about to protest. But stops herself.

"That'd be great, thanks."

[FADE TO BLACK]

🏠 Door 14 Opens: Denise – The Hustle Queen

Denise is reading a story to her kids.

She's still got some soap suds in her hair after bathtime.

She kisses them goodnight and quietly shuts their bedroom door.

Downstairs, she checks her calendar for tomorrow.

Just two meetings. One at 10 a.m. The other at 3 p.m.

She smiles. Sits on her sofa.

And allows herself to do. . . absolutely nothing.

[FADE TO BLACK]

[INT – THE WAREHOUSE]

You're back.

Future You is smiling.

FUTURE YOU:

"How do you feel?"

You're not sure how to answer.

YOU:

"I feel. . . happier. Like a weight has been lifted somehow."

Future You points to the mirror in the centre of the warehouse.

The mirror is still cracked.

You step in front of it.

You see multiple versions of yourself, but they're different to the ones you saw 66 days ago.

You see the one who's laughing while roller skating.

The one saying no to an invite when you have too much on.

The one listening to a friend with your phone out of sight.

The one turning up for the family party, gift in hand.

The one smiling as you pick up your morning coffee.

FUTURE YOU:

"It's time."

"You have to face your new future."

"To see how the consequences of your choices over the last 66 days have played out."

You swallow.

An involuntary reaction.

But you're not worried.

Future You checks a watch.

FUTURE YOU:

"See you in there."

Before you can reply, the warehouse is dissolving before your eyes.

[FADE TO BLACK]

🎭 Act III, Scene 5
The Final Verdict – Redemption

[COURTROOM – 11:58 p.m. SILENCE]

You knew you'd end up back here.

Once again, you find yourself at the back of a vast towering courtroom.

Only this time, you know why you're here.

You can see the gold stopwatch hanging by the judge's bench.

00:00:02

The face of the watch gleams.

You swear you can hear the seconds ticking down.

At **00:00:01**, Future You appears at your side.

You don't have time to greet them.

As the stopwatch hits **00:00:00**, the judge appears.

Gavel in hand.

JUDGE (echoing):

"Will the defendant please rise?"

You stand and walk forward.

"State your name for the record."

This time your voice is confident.

"66 days ago, you were charged with the following crimes. . .

- **Neglect of Self**
- **Suppression of Joy**
- **Chronic People-Pleasing**
- **Glorification of Numbness**
- **Voluntary Emotional Starvation**
- **Second-Degree Abandonment of Your Own Soul"**

"How do you plead?"

"Not guilty, your honour."

"And what evidence can you provide?"

Future You steps up.

"The following witnesses your honour. . ."

WITNESS 1: Your Family

A partner. A child. A sibling. A parent. A niece. A nephew.

Each steps up.

Eyes bright. Voice clear.

"You made time for me every day."

"You helped me with my homework each week."

"You showed up when we needed you."

"You brought laughter and joy into the house."

"You helped us connect more as a family."

WITNESS 2: Your Health

An invigorated version of your body.

"You gave me nourishing food every day."

"You used me in new and fun ways, even if I got bruised on the roller rink."

"You gave me proper rest with your new sleep routine."

WITNESS 3: Your Emotions

Resilient. Regulated. Healthy.

"You hear us and you regulate us."

"You smile in public and in private."

"You feel everything and you process us properly."

WITNESS 4: Your Mind

A gleaming processor, pulsing with energy.

"You don't just dream."

"You create."

"You think deeply and feed me positivity instead of fear."

"You have rewired me to think, create and find joy in life."

WITNESS 5: Your Spirit

Still. But strong.

A glowing human form.

"You found your safety in the silence."

"I'm your intuition."

"Your liberation."

"You choose to make time to pause."

"To listen."

"To become."

"You are becoming. . . the person you were always meant to be."

WITNESS 6: Your Future

Clean. Strong. Electric. Joyous.

"I can't wait for what's ahead."

"You've given me so much to look forward to."

"You've stepped out of comfort. And into a life less ordinary."

"I'm here, stronger than ever."

The judge rises.

FUTURE YOU:

"Wait your honour. There's more. . ."

You glance behind you.

There's a line of people walking down the courtroom aisle.

People you know.

One by one, they take the stand.

JO:

"You brought laughter and light into my weeks. Going roller skating with you gave me the confidence to start yoga classes. I'm having more fun than I have in years."

MATT:

"You listened with compassion when I needed a friend. You helped me see there was still happiness in my life. Thanks to you, I've started journaling. I'm on a journey to finding my own peace. To becoming myself again."

CHARLOTTE:

"Your determination was a joy to watch. Seeing you embrace roller skating inspired me to try something new. I'm starting life drawing classes next week."

THE NEW GUY AT WORK:

"I was on the verge of quitting that day. You don't realise what your words did. You helped me see I could turn things around. Now I've passed my probation and have a stable job to support my family."

THE BARISTA AT YOUR LOCAL COFFEE SHOP:

"Your smile cheers me up every morning. I noticed that my customers were always nicer to me after I'd served you, because I was smiling. Now I smile every day – not just at work. I pay that happiness forward."

You listen in stunned silence.

You had no idea that your redemption journey would touch others too.

Future You is grinning.

Suddenly, the courtroom is empty.

It's just you.

And the judge.

JUDGE (final):

"You thought this journey was only about you."

"But the truth is your redemption is much bigger than one person."

"It doesn't just touch your friends and family. It affects everyone you encounter."

"Now do you see why your happiness is so important?"

"It was never just about you."

A pause.

You exhale.

You hadn't even realised you were holding your breath.

JUDGE:

"I hereby sentence you to happiness."

"A life filled with laughter."

"Joy that ripples out and touches hundreds."

The gavel rises.

"You are Redeemed."

"Joy is awarded back to you."

"Use it wisely."

BANG. The gavel falls.

The courtroom dissolves.

[INT – YOUR BEDROOM – NIGHT]

You wake with a smile on your face.

It's still dark. Peaceful.

You reach for your alarm clock.

04:02.

You stretch, sigh and snuggle deeper under the duvet.

As you drift back to sleep, you're smiling.

You know tomorrow is going to be a good day.

[FADE TO BLACK]

 # Act IV
The Rebuild

This is where the real work starts. You've heard about the SMILE Framework. Seen some ways you can use it.

Now I'm going to give you your own blueprint of daily actions to help you redeem the joy in *your life*.

I know that all of our journeys are different.

So I've also got some stories to share of people who have been on their own journeys of redemption.

I want you to see that this journey is possible for you too.

No matter what your circumstances.

I've done it.

The people you'll hear from in the coming chapters have done it.

You can too.

It's time to reclaim your happiness.

Time to seek out your joy.

Time to become, so you can lead others on this quest for joy too.

# Act IV, Scene 1
The 66-Day
Redemption Challenge

The 66-Day Challenge

One Choice. One Practice. One New Identity.

By the time you reach the end of this book, you might be expecting a long list.

Sixty-six actions.

Sixty-six techniques.

Sixty-six habits to fix your life.

You're not getting that.

Not because I don't have them, but because that approach is exactly what keeps people stuck.

There's a quote by Bruce Lee that says:

> *"I am not afraid of the man who knows 10,000 kicks.*
> *I am afraid of the man who has practiced one kick 10,000 times."*

Happiness doesn't come from knowing more ideas.

It comes from **embedding one idea** so deeply that it becomes part of who you are.

The issue has never been information.

The issue has never been motivation.

The missing piece is **implementation**.

We live in a world that explains everything beautifully and applies almost nothing.

So instead of overwhelming you at the finish line, I want to do something radically simple.

I want to help you **start**.

Why 66 Days?

This challenge lasts 66 days for a reason.

Research into habit formation shows that, on average, it takes around **66 days** for a behaviour to move from effort to identity, from something you try to something you are.

Not overnight.

Not in a weekend.

Not through a motivational high.

But through repetition.

Through simplicity.

Through showing up when it feels almost too small to matter.

That's the point.

This challenge is designed to be:

- Easy to do
- Easy not to do
- Almost impossible to fail unless you don't start.

Three Options. One Commitment

At the end of this book, you don't get 66 things to do.

You get **three options**.

That's it.

You choose **one**.

And you do it **every day for 66 days**.

No switching.

No stacking.

No "I'll do all three."

This isn't about optimisation.

It's about **activation**.

Because once you prove to yourself that you can do **one simple thing consistently**, something far more important happens:

You begin to trust yourself again.

Option One: The Gratitude List

(Shifting Your State)

If I had to help someone put happiness first using just one habit, this would be it.

Gratitude.

Not because it's fashionable.

Not because it sounds spiritual.

But because it works neurologically, emotionally, and physiologically.

Gratitude has the power to:

- Shift your brainwaves
- Regulate your heart rate
- Move your nervous system out of threat mode
- Pull your attention from scarcity into abundance.

In simple terms: **gratitude changes your state**.

The Rule

For **66 days,** write down **one thing you are grateful for and why**.

That's it.

One sentence.

One reason.

You can do this either:

- First thing in the morning. . .
- Or the very last thing at night.

I personally believe the **night option is powerful,** because it frames your subconscious before sleep, but choose the time that fits your life.

Get a notepad.

Keep it by your bed.

No phone. No apps. No pressure.

"I am grateful for my wife because. . ."

"I am grateful for my dog because. . ."

"I am grateful for today because. . ."

People often say, *"I'll run out of things."*

You won't.

Your **body alone** gives you more than 66 reasons.

Your eyes. Your lungs. Your tongue. Your nervous system quietly keeping you alive.

Gratitude works best when it's **specific**.

The more granular you get, the more your system tunes into safety, sufficiency and support, and from that place, better choices naturally follow.

Option Two: The Win List (The Trophy List)

(Measuring Your Growth)

The second option is what I call **the trophy list** or the **win list**.

This is a list of things you've done.

Things you've completed.

Things you've moved forward.

Big wins or small wins all count.

Most people go through life **without ever stopping to acknowledge their progress**. They're always moving, always chasing, always focusing on what's next but never reflecting on how far they've come.

That's a problem.

Because progress that isn't recognised doesn't register emotionally.

And if your brain doesn't register progress, it doesn't release the chemicals that make you feel motivated and capable.

Why This Matters

A to-do list creates anxiety.

It releases cortisol.

A **done list** releases dopamine and serotonin.

One creates pressure.

The other creates momentum.

My Personal Example

I remember a very clear day when I woke up working from home.

The day was packed. Calls. Emails. Writing. Admin.

I was busy all day.

But by the evening, I felt unproductive like nothing had actually been done.

So I stopped and wrote down **everything I'd done that day**.

Not a to do list.

A **done list**.

As I looked over it, I literally said out loud:

"Oh. . . I *have* done some stuff today."

That moment shifted everything.

If you have a list of a thousand things to do, once you complete them, they simply give birth to more things. There is no end to your to-do list.

But your **win list** gives you closure.

Examples of wins:

- "I finally wrote that blog chapter."
- "I emptied that shelf."
- "I sent the application."
- "I hired a cleaner."
- "I had a difficult conversation."

Small wins count.

They all count.

For **66 days**, write down at least **one win per day**.

You'll start to feel progress again and progress fuels happiness.

Option Three: Seven Minutes of Silence

(Stability in a Noisy World)

The third option is more challenging but deeply powerful.

Seven minutes of silence.

We live in a world where our brains are almost never in the present.

We're in the past.

We're in the future.

We're scrolling.

We're reacting.

Silence and stillness interrupt that cycle.

When you practice silence, the first thing you discover is how noisy your mind actually is.

Thoughts bouncing around like a ping pong ball in a machine.

That's normal.

Silence doesn't stop the noise, but it allows the brain to **regulate itself**.

It grounds you.

It stabilises you.

It gives you a sense of internal control.

My Experience

The first time I tried this, I set a timer for seven minutes.

After about 60 seconds, it felt like I'd been sitting there for three hours.

It was uncomfortable.

Almost torturous.

But the more I practiced it, the better it felt.

Not quieter, just steadier.

Whenever I practice silence consistently, I feel more in control of myself.

And in a chaotic world, that's priceless.

When Do You Do This?

Let's make this as practical and as unmissable as possible.

Every option in the 66 day challenge can be completed in **seven minutes or less**.

Which means time is no longer the issue.

You have **two choices**, and you get to decide which one works best for your life:

- **First thing in the morning**
- **Or the very last thing at night**

That's it.

No "when I get around to it."

No "if I have time."

You choose a **fixed anchor point** in your day.

Morning Option

If you choose the morning, do it **before your phone**, before emails, before the world gets access to your mind.

Seven minutes.

That's all.

It sets your internal tone before the external noise arrives.

Evening Option (My Preference)

Personally, I prefer the **end of the day**.

Why?

Because the day can be rushed.

The morning can feel pressured.

But the evening allows you to **crown the day**.

These practices help you:

- Unwind the day
- Detox from mental noise
- Reset your nervous system
- Release what you're carrying.

When you end your day this way, something subtle but powerful happens: You wake up feeling lighter.

Not because life has changed. . .

but because **you've processed it**.

Whether it's gratitude, your win list, or seven minutes of silence, the evening gives you space to let the day settle rather than letting it spill into tomorrow.

No Excuses. Just a Choice

All three options:

- Fit into **seven minutes**
- Require **no equipment**
- Can be **done anywhere**
- Can be **done even on your busiest day**

So the decision isn't *whether* you can do it.

The decision is **when**.

Morning or night.

Pick one.

Anchor it.

Protect it.

Because consistency doesn't come from intensity, it comes from **simplicity**.

One Choice. Sixty-Six Days

For the next 66 days, you pick **one thing**:

- Gratitude list
- Win list
- Seven minutes of silence

And you integrate it into your life.

Nothing else.

After 66 days, you might choose another.

But first, build the **consistency muscle**.

Because once you can do one simple thing consistently, you can implement *anything*.

The Real Mirror

The mirror doesn't just show you your reflection.

It shows you your **repetition**.

You are the sum total of your habits.

By the end of these 66 days, you will feel something quietly powerful:

You voted for yourself.

You put yourself first.

You built the mechanism.

And once that mechanism exists, your desire to do more naturally increases not from pressure but from confidence.

So the choice is yours.

All the best for the next 66 days of putting your happiness first.

This is where it stops being an idea. . .

and starts becoming who you are.

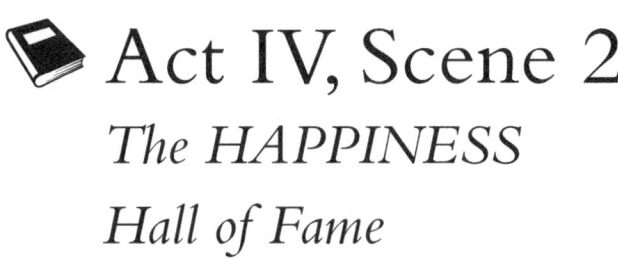

Act IV, Scene 2
The HAPPINESS Hall of Fame

In this chapter, I want to introduce you to some real people who are choosing happiness first. Their lives and stories are all very different. They're living, breathing proof that you can do this too. You can choose happiness. You can live a more fulfilled life.

Let's enter the HAPPINESS Hall of Fame. . .

HAPPINESS Hall of Fame

Name: Dr. Jazz Ampaw-Farr

What she does:

Co-founder of *Be Human First*, international keynote speaker and leadership specialist. Jazz travels the world speaking on resilience, well-being, and helping people rewrite their story so their past doesn't become their future. Alongside her husband Ed, she works with educators and executive teams to unlock human potential and build invincible cultures.

How busy she gets:

Exceptionally busy. Running a global business, raising three children, fostering medical detection dogs, navigating ADHD, and saying yes to work that feels deeply purposeful. Her work isn't just a job – it's personal, redemptive, and a way of paying forward what education once gave her.

How she puts happiness first:

Jazz doesn't try to *create* happiness – she **makes space for it**.

Her family motto is *"Add value. Bring joy."* And she lives it daily: dancing in the kitchen before school runs, turning dinner into laughter and reflection, offering small acts of kindness to strangers in airports, and choosing fun, humour, and connection on purpose.

No matter how full life gets, joy is non-negotiable.

Ironing can wait. Illness might not get scheduled.

But joy always gets a seat at the table.

Her belief is simple and powerful:

Your past does not have to be a script for your future – and the legacy worth leaving is joy.

HAPPINESS Hall of Fame

Name: Sam Spence

What she does:

Founder and CEO of *SLS360*, an inclusion and leadership consultancy working across the cultural arts, education, music, and corporate sectors. Sam supports organisations and leaders to build cultures where people feel seen, valued, and able to thrive. She is also a board chair, national leadership network founder, speaker, writer, creator, netball coach and player – and a devoted parent to a teenage daughter.

How busy she gets:

Exceptionally busy. Sam leads a national business, holds governance roles, speaks and writes regularly, coaches sport, and parents solo. In the past year, her life changed profoundly when she lost her husband and became a solo parent overnight – while continuing to lead teams, support others and show up fully. Grief didn't pause the calendar; it simply travelled with her into meetings, school runs, boardrooms and everyday life.

How she puts happiness first:

For Sam, happiness isn't about pretending everything is fine or chasing constant positivity – it's about **intentional moments of light, connection and meaning**, even when life feels heavy.

She protects joy as a **daily practice**, not a reward.

That can look like walking without her phone and truly noticing the world, immersing herself in music as a classically trained musician, moving her body through the gym, netball, or a spin class that feels like a rave. Laughter is essential – sometimes with friends, sometimes at herself, sometimes sparked by something small and unexpected.

Joy also comes from purpose. Sam chooses work that matters deeply: creating inclusive spaces, opening doors, challenging systems that cause harm and knowing that her work leaves people – especially young people – better than she found them. That sense of impact fuels happiness even on the hardest days.

She doesn't wait for life to calm down before choosing joy. She builds it deliberately into each day. Meditation, introduced by her late husband, gives her space for peace and silence – and she's learned that joy can live there too.

Her philosophy is simple and grounded:

Busy people don't need more time to be happy – they need permission to choose it.

HAPPINESS Hall of Fame

Name: Diana Osagie

What she does:

Founder and CEO of *Courageous Leadership* and the *Academy of Women's Leadership*. Diana is a former secondary headteacher, executive head, and Ofsted inspector of nine years. Today, she coaches headteachers in challenging contexts, delivers keynote speeches globally on courageous leadership, writes leadership books – with her fifth, *Juggernaut Leadership*, due in 2026 – and designs high-impact leadership development programmes for senior leaders operating under pressure.

How busy she gets:

Relentlessly busy. Diana assumed leaving headship would slow life down – it didn't. Ten years into running her own business, her days are fuller than ever. Coaching leaders one-to-one, speaking to thousands, writing books, and running development programmes leaves little space for ease. What she does is demanding, time-consuming, and often challenging – but it is deeply intentional.

How she puts happiness first:

For Diana, happiness is not something to chase – it is the natural result of **clarity and alignment**.

She is clear about her purpose: To *build platforms so other people can live triumphant lives*. Because of that clarity, happiness is not fleeting or externally driven. It doesn't depend on applause, ease, or circumstance. It flows from living in alignment with who she is and why she exists.

Every strand of her work serves that purpose.

Coaching allows her to speak directly into people's lives.

Keynotes multiply that impact at scale.

Books provide clarity people can build on.

Leadership programmes equip others to fulfil their own calling.

She learned early in business that doing work she was good at – but not called to – drained joy from her soul, even when it paid well. She made a decisive shift: She would only do work she loves, work she is excellent at, and work that aligns with her mission. The result is a life filled with joy, even when the work is hard.

Her equation is simple and uncompromising:

Clarity + alignment = happiness.

She lives this seven days a week – in her work, in service, in faith and in family. Happiness, for Diana, is not ease. It is purpose lived daily.

HAPPINESS Hall of Fame

Name: Beauty

What she does:

Project manager in the construction sector and a passionate forex trader. Beauty is an economics graduate who has intentionally built a life that blends professional structure with personal passion.

How busy she gets:

Surprisingly balanced. Beauty is busy, but never chaotic. She plans, writes things down, schedules her time, and prioritises what matters. Because of this intentional structure, life feels calm rather than overwhelming.

How she puts happiness first:

Beauty puts happiness first by **designing her life around what she loves.**

She took time to discover what brings her joy – trading, connecting with people, spending time with friends – and then built her days to support those things rather than squeeze them in as an afterthought.

Each morning, she asks herself a simple but powerful question:

What am I doing today to protect my joy?

Some days that means trading. Other days it's meeting friends, walking, or enjoying something small and light-hearted. These moments, though simple, keep her joy alive.

Happiness also comes from her environment. Being around good people, positive energy, and genuine smiles lifts her spirit. Her faith plays a central role too – putting God first brings her peace, clarity, and a sense that everything else falls into place.

For Beauty, happiness isn't loud or complicated.

It's intentional, grounded and reflected in the ease with which her smile shows up.

HAPPINESS Hall of Fame

Name: Ross McGill

What he does:

Educator, writer, researcher, and founder of *Teacher Toolkit*. Ross has spent nearly 35 years in education, beginning his teaching journey at just 18 years old and completing over 25 years in London state schools. He is an early education blogger, author of 13 books, podcaster, and international speaker, working with teachers and schools across the UK and in more than 17 countries.

Ross specialises in synthesising complex education research from Ofsted, the DfE, and neuroscience into practical, actionable ideas teachers can use immediately in the classroom. As one doctoral researcher recently described him: "A researcher who likes to teach."

How busy he gets:

Intensely busy and often stretched. Ross runs a growing education platform where much of the responsibility, income generation, and decision-making funnels through him. While supported by a team of freelancers, the pressure of sustaining the business, navigating income volatility, content saturation, algorithm shifts, and the rise of AI has been mentally demanding.

His working days are long – often 12 hours – but now more contained. Unlike his years in full-time teaching and early blogging, weekends are largely protected. The pace is still heavy, but more intentional than before.

How he puts happiness first:

Ross puts happiness first by **reintroducing structure, self-awareness, and physical well-being into a demanding life**.

After a period of struggle, he returned to what he knows best: creating a timetable. He now designs his own working week with themed days, repeatable tasks, and boundaries adjusting when school visits disrupt the rhythm, but always returning to structure. This has been essential for mental clarity and sustainability.

He actively protects well-being through daily movement, dog walks, time on the treadmill, and flexible mornings when possible. Recently, he has taken greater ownership of his health – tracking sleep, heart rate, recovery, and habits – recognising that at this stage of life, long-term well-being matters as much as output.

Happiness also comes from perspective. Ross consumes information intentionally, seeking multiple viewpoints to avoid bias, and remains deeply reflective about the future of education, content, trust, and young people in a post-AI world.

While business pressures remain real, his current strategy is simplification: fewer platforms, deeper work, long-form thinking, and a renewed focus on creating content that matters rather than chasing algorithms.

For Ross, happiness is not ease, it is **regaining control inside complexity**, staying connected to purpose, and continuing to serve teachers with integrity in a rapidly changing world.

HAPPINESS Hall of Fame

Name: Dr. Andy Cope

What he does:

First and foremost, Andy is a husband, dad, and grandad. Alongside family life, he runs a training company and spends much of his time speaking on stages of all shapes and sizes – from classrooms to boardrooms – sharing practical insights on happiness, resilience, and human flourishing.

Andy also spent a decade as a part-time researcher at Loughborough University, immersing himself in the science of happiness. After 10 years of academic work, he became the UK's first *Doctor of Happiness* – a title that may raise a smile, but underpins everything he teaches and delivers. He is also a prolific author, writing books that translate research into everyday wisdom.

How busy he gets:

Very busy but deliberately reflective about it.

Rather than competing in a busyness contest, Andy measures life differently. He tells a story – one he wrote years ago – of a father packing up his home late in life, discovering two diaries from the same period. One, his own, filled with meetings and deadlines. The other, his son's, filled with memories of joy and connection.

On one shared date, the father's diary read:

"Wasted a whole day fishing with Jimmy. Didn't catch a thing."

His son's diary read:

"Went fishing with my dad. Best day of my life."

Andy wrote that story with tears in his eyes – and made a quiet pledge: *never to become that busy.*

How he puts happiness first:

Andy puts happiness first by **refusing to treat it as a reward for success**.

Most people believe happiness comes *after* achievement – *I'll be happy when . . .*

Andy teaches the opposite: Happiness is the starting point. When people are happier, they are more productive, more successful, and more likely to thrive. Happiness fuels success not the other way around.

The single most important practice in his life is **choosing his attitude**. Not by accident, but consciously and deliberately. Andy believes attitude is something you craft and that it takes effort. Left unattended, it slips. The mind drifts into what he calls *self-imposed mental drizzle*.

By choosing a better attitude, everything changes. Nothing external shifts – but life suddenly feels lighter. Andy sometimes calls this the *Bob Marley Effect*: pause, breathe, look again. And somehow, everything's gonna be alright.

For Andy, happiness isn't something you chase.

It's something you decide – and then carry with you, every day.

Act IV, Scene 3
Final Words from Jackson

Did you notice what happened when You transformed their own happiness? It didn't just affect them. It rippled out to others.

This is the one of the most important messages: Your transformation is not only about you.

It has an impact on those around you.

Even people you might not imagine.

As you transform, subconsciously everyone around you will notice. If you stay consistent for long enough, your very presence will give other people permission to put their happiness first.

Because they've seen you do it.

Too many people in this world are so busy doing – and killing themselves in the process – that they don't realise this is killing those around them.

In liberating yourself, you're liberating others.

And this doesn't only apply to the people you encounter in this lifetime. Your ripples of happiness can spread through generations.

Imagine what you're teaching the children and young people in your life about prioritising happiness when you prioritise your own joy.

They could be your children. Or your nieces and nephews. Or your friends' kids.

If they prioritise their own happiness as they grow older, your impact will ripple out even further. You have the power to change the future.

Not just your future.

Humanity's future.

That might sound grand. But it's true. Imagine how much better the world would be if people focused less on negativity and more on happiness and joy, not just for themselves but for others.

Final Thoughts

I Am Because We Are

This entire book has been about you.

Your happiness.

Your choices.

Your habits.

Your inner world.

And yet, paradoxically, it has never been *just* about you.

Ultimately, this book is about **us**.

There is an African philosophy called *Ubuntu*, which simply means:

I am because we are.

It captures the deeper truth that while happiness begins within the individual, it is fulfilled through connection, contribution, and community.

As a speaker, trainer and pastor, I have the great privilege of helping individuals reconnect with happiness at a deep and meaningful level. And what I've observed time and time again is this: When people find that joyful space within themselves, they don't just live better lives, they create better lives for others.

Joy changes how you show up.

Fulfilment changes how you relate.

Happiness changes how you serve.

I carry a mission.

A very clear one.

To be one of the people who helped create a world where we wake up happy and go to bed fulfilled.

A world where the next generation can grow up and say,

"We are seen."

"We are protected."

"We matter."

That is the bigger picture.

For a long time in my own life, my focus was narrow.

It was me.

My goals.

My dreams.

My ambitions.

My aspirations.

And while that may sound healthy on the surface, what it actually produced was anxiety. Because when life becomes overly self-focused, it becomes heavy. Self-absorption quietly turns into pressure. Ego slowly drains energy. Obsession with self creates stress.

The shift came when I began asking a different question.

Not "What can I get from life?"

But *"How does my life add value to others?"*

And with that shift came relief.

That's why the essence of this final thought is about becoming more **allocentric**.

Allocentric simply means *other centred*.

It is the opposite of egocentric.

What drove me to search for that word was the realisation that my ego was costing me. It drained me. It took more than it gave. At certain points in my journey, it cost me relationships, both personal and professional.

So I went looking for the opposite.

And it didn't surprise me at all to discover that an allocentric life, an allocentric mindset, is the secret to deep and lasting fulfilment.

Gandhi said it best:

> *"The best way to find yourself is to lose yourself in the service of others."*

And my greatest role model and mentor, Jesus Christ, said it even more clearly:

> *"I have come that others might have life, and have it more abundantly."*

Here's the paradox.

To live an allocentric life, you must still put yourself first.

You cannot pour from an empty cup.

You cannot give joy you don't have.

You cannot model fulfilment if you are depleted.

That is why happiness first is not selfish.

It is strategic.

It is sustainable.

It is service.

So first and foremost, thank you.

Thank you for making it to this point in the book.

Thank you for staying curious.

Thank you for looking into the mirror.

Thank you for being willing to do the inner work.

We really are in this together.

Together, we can create a world filled with joyful moments.

Meaningful moments.

Moments that leave an indelible mark on our hearts.

Moments our children will look back on and build upon.

People often ask me where my energy comes from.

The truth is simple.

I am deeply connected to my belief system and my faith. My faith has been a driving force in my life. As a Christian man, I feel a responsibility, a duty, to bring light, joy and hope into the world wherever I can.

Thank you for allowing me to take you on this journey.

This cinematic, reflective, Disney-meets-therapy-meets-life-type journey.

I genuinely hope it has made an impact.

And if it has, I would love to hear from you.

Email me at Happiness@JacksonOgunyemi.com and tell me how this book has made a difference in your life.

So what's next?

Continue enjoying what you've discovered.

Continue looking into the mirror.

Continue making small tweaks that move you one step further.

Remember, we rise by lifting others.

There is profound fulfilment in seeking out another person's joy.

Because together, we are one human family.

Here's to putting happiness first.

For yourself.

And for humanity.

Thank you.

An Invitation

If this book has stirred something in you,

Made you pause,

Made you reflect,

Or gently challenged how you live, lead, or show up. . .

Then this page is for you.

This book was never meant to sit quietly on a shelf.

It was meant to start conversations.

Spark reflection.

And move happiness from theory into lived experience.

If you are a leader, whether you lead a team, a classroom, an organisation, a community, or a room full of people, and you are thinking:

"We need this conversation here."

Then let's talk.

I work with leaders and organisations across **corporate spaces, education, faith settings, and community groups**, delivering keynotes, workshops, and talks that help people reconnect with purpose, well-being, joy and sustainable performance.

Sometimes it's a full keynote.

Sometimes it's a workshop.

Sometimes it's just a conversation to explore what's possible.

There's no pressure.

No pitch.

Just connection.

And if you've read this book and simply want to tell me how it's impacted you,

What resonated,

What challenged you,

Or what you've started implementing,

I would genuinely love to hear from you.

This journey works best when it's shared.

You can reach me directly at:

Happiness@JacksonOgunyemi.com

Whether you're exploring bringing this message to your people, or you just want to say, "This helped me," my inbox is always open.

Because happiness grows when it's multiplied.

Leadership deepens when it's human.

And change happens when conversations turn into action.

Here's to continuing the journey,

Together.

Curious to know where you are on the SMILE framework? To help you, I have created an assessment you can take that will measure where you are; visit www.JacksonOgunyemi.com.

Appendices & Extras

- SMILE Framework Cheat Sheet
- Joy Meter & Dashboard Glossary
- Mirror Time Journal Prompts
- Online Directory for Interviews & Companion Video

SMILE Framework Cheat Sheet

Joy Meter & Dashboard Glossary

⌀ **Mirror Time Journal Prompts**

I've compiled all of the Mirror Time Journal Prompts from throughout the book into one place, so you can easily refer to them and use them on your journey.

? Journal Prompt

If you were put on trial for abandoning your joy. . . what would the evidence be?

Write it. Don't edit. Don't defend. Just get honest

Because this is Day 1. And this time, you get to rewrite the ending.

? Journal Prompt

What version of you is the mirror trying to show you right now?

Is it:

- The version that's burnt out, but pretending you're fine?
- The one that gives too much and receives too little?
- The one that hasn't rested properly in weeks?
- The one who is always "on," even when you're offline?
- The version who laughs out loud, but hasn't felt peace in years?

If you pay attention, really pay attention, your **future self will whisper the truth**.

? Journal Prompt

On a scale of 1 to 10. . . how much of a "yes person" are you right now?

1 = I'm comfortable saying no and setting boundaries

10 = I say yes to every request that comes my way

? Journal Prompt

On a scale of 1 to 10, how much of your identity is shaped by the need for attention or affirmation from others?

1 = My mood lives and dies on applause

10 = Internally anchored, audience irrelevant

Ask yourself:

What's the cost of constantly performing?

? Journal Prompt

On a scale of 1 to 10, how often are you present for the people who matter most?

1 = Fully available, consistently connected

10 = Routinely absent, emotionally distant

Now go deeper:

- Whose calls have you been "meaning to return"?
- When did your presence become something people have to schedule?
- What would your child, partner, parent, or best friend say about your availability?

? Journal Prompt

On a scale of 1 to 10, how connected do you feel to your body right now?

1 = Energised, grounded, physically present

10 = Sluggish, reactive, numb, or disconnected

(continued)

Now ask yourself:

- When did I stop moving my body with love?
- What story have I told myself about "not having time"?
- What kind of life do I want my body to be strong enough to carry?

? Journal Prompt

Who consistently drains my energy?

On a scale of 1 to 10, how much of your mental and emotional energy is drained by certain people in your life?

1 = Energised, clear, protected

10 = Exhausted, tense, emotionally depleted

Now go deeper:

- Whose presence consistently drains you? Write the names down. Don't edit.
- What patterns or behaviours trigger that drain?
- How often are you exposed to this energy? Daily? Weekly? Occasionally?
- What is it costing you – focus, joy, confidence, peace?
- What would shift if you reduced access by even 10% starting today?

? Journal Prompt

On a scale of 1 to 10, how often do you delay action due to overthinking?

1 = Decisive, intuitive, responsive

10 = Mentally looped, anxious, stuck in cycles

Now reflect:

- What's one thing I've been *thinking about doing* for far too long?
- What am I afraid will happen if I just. . . begin?
- What lie am I believing about "getting it perfect"?
- What would I attempt if I wasn't afraid of messing it up?

? Journal Prompt

On a scale of 1 to 10, how driven are you by the need to "get it perfect"?

1 = Grounded, progress-focused, self-compassionate

10 = Driven, anxious, highly self-critical

Now ask yourself:

- What am I afraid people will think if I don't get it right?
- What would happen if I gave myself permission to be *messy*?
- What areas of my life am I stalling on because I'm afraid of being judged?

? Journal Prompt

On a scale of 1 to 10, how much of your mental and emotional space is occupied by unresolved offence?

1 = Light, clear, emotionally free

10 = Heavy, tense, constantly replaying past hurts

(continued)

Now go deeper:

- Whose names are still on your internal ledger? Write them down. Don't censor.
- What exact moments or words still trigger a reaction in your body?
- How long have you been carrying each one? Days? Months? Years?
- What is it costing you to keep them? Energy? Relationships? Peace? Health?
- What would your life feel like if you dropped even one name from that list today?

? Journal Prompt

On a scale of 1 to 10, how much of your daily decision-making is influenced by guilt or regret?

1 = Free to act without regret pulling the strings

10 = Guided almost entirely by past mistakes

Now ask yourself:

- What memory am I still punishing myself for?
- What action have I avoided because I feel I "don't deserve" the outcome?
- If I forgave myself fully today, what would I do differently tomorrow?

? Journal Prompt

On a scale of 1 to 10, how much of what you've learned in the last six months have you actually applied?

1 = Everything I consume, I act on

10 = Mostly collecting, barely applying

Now ask yourself:

- What's one book, course, or resource I've already bought that I can act on today?
- What's stopping me from implementing it?
- What's the smallest step I can take in the next 24 hours to apply it?

? Journal Prompt

On a scale of 1 to 10, how often do you find yourself comparing your life to others (online or offline)?

1 = I stay in my lane and clap for others genuinely

10 = I can't scroll for five minutes without spiralling

? Journal Prompt

On a scale of 1 to 10, how much of your day is spent repeating what's wrong. . . vs resolving it?

1 = Solution-driven and energised

10 = Certified moaner with a PhD in pessimism

? Journal Prompt

On a scale of 1 to 10, how much are you currently carrying alone that could be shared?

1 = Delegating like a boss

10 = Martyr mode: full activation

(continued)

? Journal Prompt

On a scale of 1 to 10, how glorified is "being busy" in your life?

1 = I honour rest, boundaries, and presence

10 = If I stop moving, I panic

Now ask yourself:

- What *real* emotions am I avoiding by staying constantly busy?
- What's one thing I can say "no" to this week without the world falling apart?
- If I stopped equating busyness with worth. . . what would change?

? Journal Prompt

Out of the 14 doors. . .

Which three felt most familiar?

Why?

Online Directory for Interviews and Companion Video

To really bring the Happiness First journey to life, visit my website, where you'll find companion video content that goes alongside this book, interviews, and other resources to support you as you consciously bring more joy into your life.

www.JacksonOgunyemi.com

About the Author

Jackson Ogunyemi, aka Action Jackson, "UK Ambassador for Happiness," is a motivational speaker.

What Sets Him Apart?

Action Jackson isn't just a speaker, he's an experience. Known for his E4 Method – a unique mix of Energy, Entertainment, Empowerment, and Education – he goes beyond traditional keynotes to deliver a captivating performance. Whether playing the guitar, weaving in stand-up comedy, or using powerful storytelling, he ensures every moment is engaging, memorable, and impactful. With his background in NLP (Neuro-Linguistic Programming), he crafts messages that deeply connect, inspiring audiences to take bold action.

Inspiring Transformation, Delivering Results, and Energising Audiences Worldwide

Action Jackson is one of the UK's most sought-after corporate speakers, known for his dynamic energy, humour, and ability to leave a lasting impact. With over 25 years of experience and more than 1,500 talks delivered to CEOs, entrepreneurs, and leaders across the globe, he has become a trusted name for organisations looking to inspire change and achieve extraordinary results.

Clients and Impact

Jackson has worked with some of the world's leading organisations, including Google, Amazon, McDonald's, LinkedIn, Boeing, AstraZeneca, NHS, Veolia, Johnson & Johnson, GE Aerospace, and ITV. His sessions ignite motivation, build resilience, and equip audiences with actionable insights to thrive in today's fast-paced environment.

Described by Simon Cowell as "an unstoppable force for happiness," Action Jackson has the rare ability to combine wit, wisdom, and high-energy delivery to create transformative experiences that resonate with audiences long after the event.

Signature Keynote

- **Motivation:** Inspiring individuals and teams to push boundaries, overcome challenges, and unlock their full potential with actionable strategies and "contagious energy."
- **Happiness:** Helping individuals and teams create lasting joy and fulfilment, spreading contagious positivity throughout the organisation.
- **Leadership and Well-Being:** Equipping leaders with tools to balance mental and physical well-being, fostering sustainable success and resilience.
- **Inspiration:** Sparking innovation and action by unlocking the potential within individuals and teams.

You can connect with me on socials
Instagram, TikTok, YouTube, X
@ActionJacksonlive
Facebook Jackson Ogunyemi
LinkedIn Jackson Ogunyemi
Text Me: +447494 197 184

Index